Maurice Duplessis, 1890-1959.

Illustration: Francine Auger.

Marguerite Paulin

Marguerite Paulin produces and hosts her own radio show in Montreal at Radio Centre-Ville, on which she interviews writers. She has a doctorate (arts), has lectured for ten years at McGill University, and has taught at the collegiate level as well. She is the author of three other biographies – *Louis-Joseph Papineau*, *René Lévesque*, and *Félix Leclerc*. She has also published essays and fiction.

The translator: Nora Alleyn

Nora Alleyn grew up in a bicultural family in Quebec City. After a B.A. from McGill University (languages), and diplomatic postings in Europe and the Middle East, she returned to Montreal where she worked for many years at the National Film Board of Canada as a staff writer and translator. She now works almost exclusively as a literary translator.

In the same collection

Maurice Duplessis

Library and Archives Canada Cataloguing in Publication
Paulin, Marguerite, 1955-
Maurice Duplessis: powerbroker, politician

(The Quest library; 26)

Translation of: Maurice Duplessis: Le noblet, le petit roi.
Includes bibliographical references and index.
ISBN 1-894852-17-6

1. Duplessis, Maurice, 1890-1959. 2. Québec (Province) – Politics and government – 1936-1960. 3. Prime ministers – Québec (Province) – Biography. I. Alleyn, Nora. II. Title. III. Series: Quest library; 26.

FC2924.1.D86P3813 2005   971.4'04'092   C2005-941665-3

Legal Deposit: Third quarter 2005
Library and Archives Canada
Bibliothèque nationale du Québec

XYZ Publishing acknowledges the support of The Quest Library project by the Book Publishing Industry Development Program (BPIDP) of the Department of Canadian Heritage. The opinions expressed do not necessarily reflect the views of the Government of Canada.

The publishers further acknowledge the financial support our publishing program receives from The Canada Council for the Arts, the ministère de la Culture et des Communications du Québec, and the Société de développement des entreprises culturelles.

Chronology: Michèle Vanasse
Index: Darcy Dunton
Layout: Édiscript enr.
Cover design: Zirval Design
Cover illustration: Francine Auger
Photo research: Anne-Marie Sicotte and Marcel Brouillard

Printed and bound in Canada

XYZ Publishing
1781 Saint Hubert Street
Montreal, Quebec   H2L 3Z1
Tel: (514) 525-2170
Fax: (514) 525-7537
E-mail: info@xyzedit.qc.ca
Web site: www.xyzedit.qc.ca

Distributed by: Fitzhenry & Whiteside
195 Allstate Parkway
Markham, ON L3R 4T8
Customer Service, tel: (905) 477-9700
Toll free ordering, tel: 1-800-387-9776
Fax: 1-800-260-9777
E-mail: bookinfo@fitzhenry.ca

International Rights: Contact André Vanasse, tel. (514) 525-2170 # 25
E-mail: andre.vanasse@xyzedit.qc.ca

MARGUERITE PAULIN

Maurice Duplessis

POWERBROKER, POLITICIAN

XYZ
Publishing

In memory of my father,
my dear mother,
my nephew Alexis,

and, of course, to Victor-Lévy Beaulieu.

"We were a people hungry for
legitimacy. We accepted power
as long as it meant absolute Power,
regardless of outcome.
Our drive for power was constant."

Paul Chamberland, *De la damnation à la liberté*

"It's difficult to define how we must keep the faith.
History only provides us with
certain signs, certain arguments.
But an argument is not truth per se,
only a way of looking at things.
History has no purpose other than to defend a cause.
The important thing is to know what cause
we are defending."

Pierre Perrault, *Un pays sans bon sens*

Contents

Preface

The name Maurice Duplessis will always spark debate. To some, he is Quebec's greatest premier. To others, he will always be a tyrant, a fascist.

This biographical narrative does not set out either to judge or to exonerate him. Others before me have taken sides. Others after me will take sides. But not everything has been said about Duplessis.

In order to write this book, I needed to research his life. I followed his traces – the traces of a man who figured so prominently in Quebec's political history. My research revealed the dark recesses of his personality before the man gradually evolved into the politician he became.

Since I had no wish to write either an apologia or a pamphlet, I tried to observe strict impartiality. My sole objective was to revive the story of the politician who was the longest-governing premier in Quebec's history.

Here is the book, which I give you to read – in all simplicity.

Who was Maurice Duplessis? The answer can be summed up in the words of French author/philosopher

Jean-Paul Sartre: "A man is made up of all men, is equal to all of them just as they are equal to him."

– Marguerite Paulin

1

This Young Man Will Go Far

When asked what name he would choose for his child, Nérée Duplessis answered:

"Maurice, if it's a boy. Do you know why? To honour the people in the riding of Saint-Maurice, because that's where I was first elected to the Quebec legislature in 1886 – and I hope to represent them for as long as I can."

On April 20, 1890, two months before his re-election to the Legislative Assembly,[1] Conservative politician Nérée Duplessis hands out cigars to his friends. His wife, Berthe Genest, has just given birth to a strapping baby boy. The family's first son cries in his

1. The Quebec Legislative Assembly was renamed the "National Assembly" in 1968.

Berthe Genest, mother
of Maurice Duplessis

Nérée Duplessis,
father of Maurice Duplessis,
around 1895.

Maurice Duplessis,
around 1908, a young law student
at the Université Laval of Montreal.

crib. He is hungry, and he is thirsty. Bursting with pride, a jubilant Nérée mingles with his guests. The family lineage is assured.

"Look! My son is already an orator. Just listen to him! He insists on being heard. He's already showing character. A real Duplessis."

Berthe swaddles her infant.

She thinks of her neighbours who have just lost a newborn. The health of an infant is so fragile. The remedies against contagious diseases are not very effective. The christening must take place soon as possible. If something should happen to the little boy, at least he will not end up in Limbo.

The city of Trois-Rivières is Bishop Laflèche's kingdom, especially when he preaches fire and brimstone from the pulpit: the sky is *bleu*[1], hell is *rouge*[2]. Formerly a missionary in the Canadian West, the prelate with the flashy reputation has returned to Quebec to preach ultramontanism, a movement that advocates the supremacy of Church over State. His most fervent political mouthpiece is Nérée Duplessis who, in the spirit of reciprocity, benefits from Bishop Laflèche's influence over his parishioners. He is re-elected virtually without opposition in his home riding.

The two make quite the pair.

So it is only natural that Bishop Laflèche should bless the son of the honourable member for Saint-Maurice. When his godmother holds the wriggling newborn above the baptismal font, the prelate, lost in

1. Conservative.
2. Liberal.

prayer, administers the sacrament: *Vade retro, Satana.* Then, with a solemn gesture, he makes the sign of the cross on the baby's forehead. "I baptize thee, Joseph Maurice Le Noblet Duplessis, in the name of the Father, the Son, and the Holy Ghost."

Nérée and Berthe feel at peace. Their child is now a son of the Catholic religion.

Nothing can cloud their happiness.

∞

In Trois-Rivières, the Duplessis family enjoys the prestige of being comfortably off. Son of the Conservative member, Maurice lacks for nothing. In winter, he cavorts on the skating rink. He plays hockey sporting a brand-new sweater and skates. In summer, he runs to the baseball field in knickerbockers, with the proper leather glove on his hand. On Sundays, the whole family occupies the front pew in their parish church.

The years pass in peaceful serenity, but a dark shadow hovers in the background. There are days when Nérée is haunted by the unthinkable. Could he one day lose the election? With Honoré Mercier in power, the member for Saint-Maurice pulls out all the stops against the despised enemy. He attacks ferociously, like Caton the Ancient against Carthage:

"They're all rotten, the Rouges! And this Mercier, what a scoundrel! He has so much money that he built himself a mansion out in the country while our poor farmers are starving."

The departure of the head of the Liberal Party gives new impetus to the Duplessis family for whom politics is the mainstay of their existence. Maurice, constantly overhearing his father's propaganda, picks up his words: "They're all rotten, those Rouges!" This makes his parents laugh. Eventually, might he not also represent the riding? A future premier, perhaps?

In 1897, Nérée fights yet another electoral campaign like a soldier in the line of fire. Maurice loves accompanying him. Sometimes, he even improvises short harangues in support of his father. One day, he slips into the crowd gathered around the podium not far from the church and the small restaurant where they sell penny candy.

"Go and pass around these pamphlets to those who seem less interested, and also to the women. They don't vote but they can influence their husbands," Nérée tells his son before climbing up onto the podium. He is determined to point out the broad lines of his platform while reviling liberalism, branding it a social plague.

But his adversaries are tough. Some of them have even stormed the square. Maurice can't believe it. They are heckling his father and shouting hostile slogans: "You're a traitor, Nérée. The Bleus are scoundrels, rogues!"

What is the meaning of these words? Since John A. Macdonald agreed to the hanging of Louis Riel, the Conservative Party bears the blame for this emblematic death. Luckily for the Duplessis family, the Saint-Maurice riding is Conservative through and through. In May 1897, Nérée is re-elected member of the Quebec legislature but this time he has to sit in the Opposition. Liberal Félix-Gabriel Marchand has won fifty-one seats against twenty-three Conservatives.

Maurice is the only boy in a family of five children. Mischievous, spoiled by his sisters Etiennette, Marguerite, Gabrielle, and Jeanne, he knows they will always forgive him his pranks. One day at mealtime, his father, losing patience, orders him abruptly:

"Maurice, stop being so silly at the table!"

Instead of stopping, the young boy gets up and answers back:

"There! Now I can go on... I'm no longer at the table."

Maurice is very amusing. He knows how to win people. His mother makes a fuss over him. His sisters lavish affection on him. Nérée says of his eight-year-old son that he is a troublemaker, like his ancestors. "He'll go far. He's not afraid of discipline." When it's time to think about his education, his parents choose one of the best schools for this lively and resourceful boy. It is autumn of 1898. Maurice Duplessis is enrolled as a student at Collège Notre-Dame, Montreal.

Montreal seems to be at the other end of the world. The first few weeks are very difficult for the young boarder – the long corridors, the dark dormitory, the classrooms with their blackboards. From the window of the refectory, the boy tries to glimpse the blue of the sky poking through the trees. The school, run by the Brothers of the Holy Cross congregation, is located in Notre-Dame-des-Neiges, a rather remote spot but recently accessible by tramway. The landscape, with Mount Royal right across from the college, reminds him of the Mauricie region.

Maurice Duplessis is an obedient pupil who works hard to obtain good marks. His notebooks are filled with expressions of praise, stamps, and stars; his report cards are satisfactory. He looks like a model pupil dressed in a blue blazer with brass buttons, short pants, and a white shirt with a hard collar. In June, when the prizes are handed out, he doesn't mind if he is not first in all subjects. What is important is his parents' presence in the hall. And knowing that he will spend the summer in Trois-Rivières. At last, he will be able to play baseball with Paul, Robert, and Jean, his little neighbours from Hart Street whom he hasn't seen for ten months.

∞

At Collège Notre-Dame, there is someone who performs miracles!

Maurice comes home full of stories about his life in Montreal. His mother listens to him. He tells her that one day, as he was walking down the corridor, he noticed a strange little man with a threadbare cassock.

"Everyone calls him the 'greasy brother' because he helps cure wounds with oil. But I call him by his real name: Brother André. And he's a friend."

Brother André is very devout, humble. He reminds Maurice of people he knows in Trois-Rivières. He has the same humility and generosity of spirit. Brother André is the college doorman. Often he is tired after his long day. To help him, Maurice offers to fetch the pupils and bring them to the common room. From then on, they become close. The child admires the Brother who speaks of St. Joseph like a friend.

"You know, Mother, Brother André says that one day he will have an oratory built on Mount Royal in honour of his patron saint, Joseph. Many people laugh at him but I don't. I'm sure he'll succeed."

He admires such determination. Maurice is discovering the mysterious power that this humble man exercises over others. A kind of charisma. It fascinates him.

After he graduates from Collège Notre-Dame, Maurice continues his classical studies at the Trois-Rivières Seminary. Even though he is only a teenager, people are already taking notice of his talent as an orator.

"Why not come to the Saint-Thomas-d'Aquin Academy?" a friend asks one day. "You like history and politics. I listened to your arguments about the Boer War and they were very convincing. You can take part in the debates we are organizing around certain themes. Next week, it will be Lincoln and the War of Secession. We need someone who will defend the Confederates. It's a thankless role, but I can see you standing up for those who have been defeated."

What an opportunity! Maurice is enthusiastic. He joins this group of young people who engage in spirited verbal matches. Elegant in his three-piece suits, with a trim moustache and his hair slicked back, he is impressive. And when he participates in the debates, he stirs up the audience. He soon stands out from the group.

"Who is that boy who speaks so well?"

"He's the son of Nérée Duplessis, the former representative for Saint-Maurice. Watch him, he'll go far, this young man. They say he can't be beaten when it comes to politics."

His reputation grows. His father, who holds a salon, introduces him to his friends, well-known members of the Conservative Party. Maurice talks about current affairs with historian-politician Thomas Chapais and two former premiers, Louis-Olivier Taillon and Edmund James Flynn. The year is 1908 and Trois-Rivières is slowly recovering from the great fire of June 22. Rumour says that the fire started in a stable with horses for hire. It spread like wildfire, destroying the centre of town. The business sector, the post office, the offices of the Canadian Pacific Railway, the beautiful parish church – a whole architectural heritage turned to ashes. The fire couldn't have happened at a worse time. Industrialization had just started to draw rural families into the towns. But Trois-Rivières cannot compete with Montreal and Quebec City. Maurice reassures Thomas Chapais, who is worried about how the region will develop. He tells him that neither the Wabasso Cotton Company nor the Shawinigan Water and Power Company are about to leave town. And that reconstruction will help modernize their small city.

"Trois-Rivières, with the help of American capital, can become the new economic centre of Quebec," says Maurice. "We have the forests for logging and the factories for producing pulp and paper. Loggers and workers come from everywhere to work here in the Mauricie region. And we are at midpoint on the river, which gives us the most sought-after resource in the twentieth century: electricity. The Shawinigan Power Company is our trump card. The fire is out; water is our future."

Maurice's intuition is accurate. He understands the challenge of the future. When he speaks, it's easy to imagine that one day he will run for office.

"But I'm not even old enough to vote yet. First, I want to study law at Université de Laval in Montreal."

His career plan is simple: finish his legal studies and then return to Trois-Rivières to open his own law practice. Maurice intends to climb the rungs of the profession step by step. And afterwards? When he is admitted to the Bar, there will be time enough to redirect his life. He doesn't hide his ambitions, but he wants to consolidate his chances and learn the rules of the game before going into battle. Easy does it. This young man is not in a hurry. For the moment, he is busy making contacts and asking advice from his elders.

During a political meeting, he talks to Louis-Olivier Taillon, the patriarch with the white beard and the easygoing manner who seems to incarnate a wise man. Despite being defeated several times, the man's authority has never been questioned. The elderly politician, feeling nostalgic, casts his mind back to the ultramontane movement. Ah! Those were wonderful times when the Zouaves marched to save the Pope. In 1868, one hundred and thirty-five volunteers left from Bonaventure Station, feeling brave and bold.

"Remember, Maurice, our faith and our language have saved the French-Canadian people. In politics, the Church is our ally. The Conservatives' strength is based on the respect for tradition. The Liberals like to show off their great orators like Ernest Lapointe, but you'll see, one day we'll be back in power."

Young Duplessis's reply is lively and prompt:

"I also believe that. Henri Bourassa wants to be our new saviour, but Louis-Joseph Papineau's grandson is in fact an imposter. On today's political stage, the head of the nationalist movement doesn't measure up. As for Lomer Gouin, he's a Liberal with an eye on Ottawa. He is betting on both sides. We just have to be patient. The Conservative Party will rise from the ashes, believe me. It is never as much alive as when everyone is singing its swan song."

∞

The young man turns onto Saint-Hubert Street by way of Sherbrooke Street. Université Laval, located in the heart of the Latin quarter, is farther down Saint-Denis Street. This evening, Maurice is meeting friends at the Ouimetoscope movie house. They are showing the documentary *Chutes du Niagara en hiver* [Niagara Falls in Winter] and the silent film *Le papillon humain* [The Human Butterfly]. A novelty. Movies are in fashion and the archbishop of Montreal is starting to be wary of this kind of entertainment on a Sunday. But for the moment, at the corner of Montcalm and Sainte-Catherine streets, Maurice slips into the theatre along with the rest of the crowd. On the verge of obtaining his law degree, he cuts a fine figure. He is wearing a suit with a matching tie and breast pocket hanky. His hair is slicked back with perfumed pomade, and he sports a well-trimmed moustache. Son of a bourgeois family, he is a member of the privileged class. He exudes the good manners of his family. During a recent "model parliament" organized by the students of the law faculty and staged at the Monument National Theatre, he impressed his fellow students. He has talent, especially as a public speaker. He can control any audience. And he knows how to hold their attention.

"He is charismatic," someone remarked. "The only problem is, he knows it."

∞

Before being admitted to the Bar in September 1913, Maurice Duplessis articles in Montreal in the offices of Monty & Duranleau, friends of his father's. With them he is free to discuss legal affairs and political ideas. The two old-timers from the Bleus are furious at seeing the rising popularity of Nationalist leader Henri Bourassa who, in January 1910, founded the newspaper, *Le Devoir*. He is a pundit. When he speaks in the name of the French-Canadian nation, one can hear the voice of his ancestor, Papineau, leader of the Patriots of 1837. Duplessis, amused, watches this new leader of the defrocked ones from the past: "He makes me think of the *Titanic* that sank last year: a big ship that boasted it was unsinkable and was destroyed by an iceberg."

Maurice, very perceptive, understands that French Canadians need political heroes. Since Confederation, it has always been the great orators who have defended the bastion of the French-Canadian nation threatened by assimilation. In Ontario, Bill 17, which declared English as the only language in the schools, cranked up Quebec patriotism by a notch. *This is where the battle lies*, thinks the young man. A wise decision, made at a time when those who want to run for office hesitate between Ottawa and Quebec City.

Prior to 1874, several politicians chose to represent both a federal and a provincial riding. Louis-Olivier Taillon, at the time leader of the Conservative Party and former premier of Quebec, had also been an MP in Ottawa, and even minister of postal services in the Tupper cabinet. But Maurice Duplessis is convinced Quebec is the battleground where the political rights of the French Canadians must be defended.

Already, at twenty-three, he is telling his friends that one day, he will run for office. But he doesn't want to throw himself into the arena like a rookie, without experience or the necessary preparation. He wants to take the time to study the plans, tactics, and strategies of the Liberals and the Nationalists. He believes that one should never underestimate one's adversaries. To win, one needs time – and he is patient.

These are troubled times. Maurice follows closely what is happening around the world. He reads the newspapers. Small conflicts are breaking out all over the planet, like in the Balkans. But these events happening so far away are of little concern to him. Robert Borden, the Conservative who won against Wilfrid Laurier, has been directing the destiny of the country since 1911. Canada is coping pretty well with its internal problems. Life goes on, with its highs and its lows, without too many problems. Today the weather is beautiful. On Sainte-Catherine Street, it is the end of June and already summer. By chance, he bumps into a friend.

"Did you hear the news? The Archduke of Austria, Crown Prince Franz Ferdinand, has just been assassinated."

∞

"It's a long way to Tipperary, it's a long way to go…"

It is Sunday afternoon. The gramophone needle slides along the grooves of the record. Maurice is in his parents' parlour. He and his father are talking about Trois-Rivières, Montreal, and the events that have inflamed the planet. It has been more than two years since Canada entered the First World War on the side of Great Britain. The war is dragging on. Who would have thought that the shot fired by terrorist Gavrilo Princip on June 28, 1914 against Franz Ferdinand, Archduke and heir to the throne of the Austro-Hungarian empire, would have plunged so many countries into fire and bloodshed?

"What a shame that Borden had to pass a law on conscription," confides Maurice to his father. "Once again, French Canadians will criticize their government for having duped them. In Ottawa, the government had promised that it would send only volunteers. Quebecers won't soon forget that it was the Bleus who forced unmarried men to sign up."

"Particularly since the province clearly voted against conscription. The Conservatives are only just recovering from their blunder in the Louis Riel affair and they are once again showing their contempt of French Canadians."

"Yesterday I saw our young neighbour who was called up and has to report to Montreal next week. He is leaving to go halfway around the world. This will be the first time he crosses the Atlantic, and it is to go and fight… And he's just eighteen."

Maurice is certain that the entry of the United States into the war will hasten the end of the struggle. At least that is what he hopes. Even though he is not afraid of going to the front – as a professional he is exempt – he has seen pictures in the newspapers of mutilated *poilus*[1] and young men lying in the trenches on their bayonets. It's a dirty war. Although his own law practice is going well, the mood everywhere is dark.

Nérée guesses that his son is hiding something from him. Getting up, he walks to the window. Turning his back on Maurice, he speaks in stinging tones:

"I heard that you're seeing young Augustine Delisle. Tell me: what does her father do?"

The answer is long in coming. The silence is heavy.

"I think he sells coal."

How can the son of the former MLA who has become a judge, Nérée Duplessis's only son, become involved with the daughter of a coal merchant?

"Listen, Maurice! Have you thought what people will say about you? About us? And when you have children? A lawyer with the daughter of a coal merchant! What a dishonour for the family!"

The argument dies out. A knife has been driven into his illusions, his dreams, his love. If Maurice insists on courting Augustine, he had better know once and for all, the Duplessis family will never agree to such a union. There is no question of going against his father's authority. Marriage is a very big commitment. Will he

1. French nickname for a soldier who fought in the First World War (1914-18).

have enough time for family life? And is that what he really wants?

Politics is what interests him more and more. He wants to dedicate himself with more rigour, more seriousness. The First World War is about to turn the universe upside down. When German cannons are finally silenced, when our soldiers finally come back, Canada and Quebec will have been transformed. A new society will rise up out of the old one. The young man feels ready to step out from the wings. He wants to play a leading role at the Legislative Assembly. Love can wait. Augustine is a fine girl, and one day she will find a fine young man and have children. Nérée settles into his armchair:

"Put another record on the gramophone."

Maurice adjusts the speaker and, without even looking, almost as if by accident, he plays a love ballad full of hope:

La Madelon pour nous n'est pas sévère
Quand on lui prend la taille ou le menton
Elle rit, c'est tout l'mal qu'elle sait faire
Madelon, Madelon, Madelon
[Madelon is never strict with us
When we take her by the waist or cup her chin
She just laughs, she's never mean
Madelon, Madelon, Madelon]

2

"Time and Patience..."

In Trois-Rivières, the young neighbourhood lawyer is making a name for himself. For him, no case is too trivial. One day, a homeowner comes to see him:

"Sir, I mean Maître Duplessis! I knew your father well. Ah! what a great MLA he was! I need your help because I'm having problems with my new neighbour. He has built a fence on my land. It just happened and he thinks he can get away with it!"

In his office on Hart Street, a kindly, attentive Maurice Duplessis treats people like his friends. Well up on municipal, school, and parish affairs, he is the one whom people recommend to settle property disputes or wills, and quarrels over land or codicils. Are not his customers future voters? He is building a

Maurice Duplessis becomes a lawyer
and is admitted to the Bar on September 14, 1913.

network of supporters. Their contributions will be useful; their vote will be his capital. For example, if an old parishioner comes complaining to him that somebody stole his chickens, Maître Duplessis receives him courteously. "Please be seated, Sir," he'll say pleasantly. "I will take them to court, those thieves. I promise you they will have to face justice."

People trust Maurice Duplessis because he is a winner. In court, he speaks loud and clear. His arguments are based on plain common sense. His waiting room soon fills up. The more impatient ones try to meet Maurice before he goes to his office. Every morning, around eight, he picks up his mail at the post office. Maurice speaks to everyone, he likes to joke, to laugh at life's little problems. His reputation as the defender of the widow and the orphan grows. Those who have seen him plead say that his cases are like theatre. His defence is great oratory. Sometimes, he even has the judge in tears:

"Your Honour, look at this brave man, a farmer who has given his life to feed his family. Do you think for one moment that he would steal his grandfather's inheritance?"

But, more often than not, lawyer Maurice Duplessis entertains the gallery with his puns and jests. The judges are fond of him. He is very talented. His theatrical arm-waving is well calculated to hold his audience in sway. He reserves the right word for his offensive, and then explodes with an irresistible witticism. He learns to dominate a crowd, to win over the undecided at the Bar, at the Court House. The courtroom is where he is sharpening his political skills.

Maurice Duplessis doesn't only defend the man in the street. He also represents the corporations of the region, like the Shawinigan Water and Power Company. Over the years, he makes friends everywhere. His name is synonymous with success, especially in cases of civil law, which interests him passionately. When asked if he would eventually go in for criminal law, he answered that he would find it extremely disagreeable having to defend a murderer.

In the meantime, newspapers are having a field day with the trial of Télesphore Gagnon's wife from Lotbinière. Marie-Anne Houde is accused of having brutalized her stepdaughter, poor little Aurore, who has died as a result of her injuries. The trial has sparked a great deal of curiosity verging onto voyeurism, and has turned into a veritable circus. The crowd is jostling to get a good look at the stepmother and to listen to the deliberations. Maurice Duplessis's cases pale by comparison to this soap opera. And yet each victory in the court of law brings him closer to his ultimate goal: politics.

Since Msgr. Laflèche's death in 1898, Jacques Bureau, a Liberal, is the new strongman in Trois-Rivières. He reigns over it as if it were his personal fiefdom. Appointed solicitor general by Wilfrid Laurier, he enjoys enormous prestige. It was he who gave the Rouges the seat everyone thought was painted blue forever. Maurice has not forgotten the time when his father was the Conservative deputy for the region. Maybe the time has come to get even and give Bureau's gang a good lesson.

"The election is coming. Why not try our luck?" asks Arthur Sauvé, new head of Quebec's Conservative

Party. He is looking for good candidates for the February 5, 1923 election.

Maurice Duplessis's qualifications are impeccable. He is young, dynamic, a brilliant lawyer whose good name is an added plus. Two years earlier, at the federal election, he had agreed to work for the Conservative candidate despite the anti-conscription attacks directed at the Bleus. So he also has courage. His political allegiances are well known. That is why Arthur Sauvé urges him to come to Montreal and meet him. Flattered, Duplessis doesn't hesitate for very long. In Sauvé's office, the two men have much to talk about.

"My dear Maurice, in Quebec, we are stagnating in the Opposition because of that old goat Taschereau who puts the good people of the province to sleep. I dream of the day when we can dislodge him. I feel that you have the potential to take on this Herculean task."

"I don't think I have any chance of winning. The people of Trois-Rivières are not yet ready to let go of Bureau, who strokes them the right way."

"I want to renew my team," says Sauvé. "In Montreal, I found Camillien Houde, an ex-bank employee and insurance salesman, a working-class man. The big city has had enough of Quebec potentates. I think that in your town, there is a similar undercurrent of dissatisfaction. I'm convinced that you could channel these feelings in your favour. Come on, jump into the fray. I have great confidence in you."

Maurice Duplessis doesn't need to be begged for long. He has considered his chances. Even though they are slight, he decides to take the leap. He is resigned to losing. So, on the evening of February 5, after

Camillien Houde's victory in Sainte-Marie is announced, the vote-counting is a simple formality. The outcome is as predicted. The Liberal opponent is re-elected deputy by a majority of two hundred votes.

It is Maurice Duplessis's first electoral defeat. And his last as candidate for the riding of Trois-Rivières. *Next time will be the right time*, he tells himself. When he goes back to the electorate, it will be to keep them "in his pocket" for the next three decades.

∞

Auréa Cloutier has heard about a secretarial position in a lawyer's office. Born in Iron Mountain, Michigan, she moved to Trois-Rivières with her parents when she was five. She speaks French and writes it almost perfectly. Wearing a pearl-grey suit, gloves, and a small felt hat, she presents herself at the Hart Street office.

"I'm almost thirty years old, and I wonder if I'm too old."

Maurice Duplessis sizes her up. This young lady looks serious. Is she discreet? It is very important that she know how to keep secrets, that she be meticulous. A trustworthy, devoted secretary.

"Miss Auréa Cloutier, I'm hiring you. On a trial basis for one week. I will keep you on if I'm satisfied with your work. One of your jobs will be to cut out any newspaper articles about me. You will put them in this file, at the end of my desk."

The pact is concluded: the two are united, more faithful than if they were married. Over time, Auréa

Cloutier will go from being a legal secretary to his political attaché. She is the one who greets Maître Duplessis's clients. Gradually, she gets to know better than anyone else the friends of the Conservative Party. If Mr. So-and-So is more important, he is admitted before the one who is a Liberal. And does he contribute to the electoral kitty of the Bleus? Then she treats him like a prince. He is entitled to treatment commensurate with his generosity.

One day, Maurice Duplessis leaves a book that he has borrowed from the library on his secretary's desk. "Miss Cloutier," he says in a firm voice, "copy the passage on the Workers' Compensation Act in Russia."

Why all this zeal? Everything is useful to Duplessis if he wants to become MLA for Trois-Rivières. The day after his defeat in the election of 1923, Maurice starts to rally his supporters. He puts together a plan based on the needs of his riding. At the next election, in four years, he knows he will be ready to face any kind of adversary. To temper any outburst of impatience, he recalls a fable by La Fontaine, whose tales he often memorized when he was at the Collège Notre-Dame. The fable is *The Lion and the Rat*. And so, quite naturally, he thinks of the moral of the fable: "Patience and hard work do more than strength or rage."

The two major political parties are playing musical chairs at the federal and provincial levels. Canadians go to the polls in 1925. The election campaign is a lacklustre one as Liberal William Lyon Mackenzie King hangs on to the power coveted by Conservative Arthur Meighen. Maurice Duplessis remains on the sidelines.

He waits for his turn. He is helping out a friend in Berthier, but he doesn't think it wise to throw himself into the fray just yet.

Surprisingly, what he waxes most enthusiastic about is a new machine that he has just bought: a wireless radio that he installs in the middle of his living room. On October 29, comfortably seated and surrounded by friends, he listens for the first time to the results of the election over the wireless. A technical revolution! Surrounded by friends, Maurice uses this opportunity to poke fun at the federal leader:

"Poor old Mackenzie King, he consults Mrs. Bleaney, his fortune teller, but he's not able to win a convincing victory. You don't need a crystal ball to see that Wilfrid Laurier's successor hasn't the stuff to be his heir!"

For Duplessis, the quarrels in Ottawa are like quarrels among distant cousins. He chooses to invest his energy into what is going on in Quebec. He follows the news avidly, reads several newspapers a day and listens faithfully to his wireless. He already appreciates that this medium can be a powerful ally if you know how to use it properly. Voters can be reached in their own homes. Yes, this is how the politician must appeal to the population and invite them to vote for him.

Talk, discuss, joke – who better than flamboyant lawyer Maurice Duplessis can do all this and seduce his listeners?

It is only a question of time. Soon, most Quebecers will turn on their radios and listen to the future MLA from Saint-Maurice convincing them to place their trust in him.

∞

"Miss Cloutier, I'm off to New York for a few days. If you come across an article about Camillien Houde, put it in my files. And find out if there is any connection between the Taschereau family and the Banque canadienne nationale of Donnacona. And don't forget to send a birthday card to Mrs. Crépeau. She is a good friend of the Conservatives."

Growing up, Maurice Duplessis used to play in the parks of Trois-Rivières. He has turned into an ardent baseball fan. He can reel the statistics off by heart, and he knows the strengths and weaknesses of each player. When he attends the games, he can predict their strategy of attack and defence.

"Baseball is like the all-American dream," he says to his friends. "The players are workers on a huge field. It is the only sport where statistics are averaged and the referees are so important." The Yankees are Duplessis's favourite team. When he can get tickets, he goes to New York to watch his hero play, the hero of a whole generation: George Herman "Babe" Ruth. The great Babe, with his Louisville Slugger, who hit sixty home runs in one year. Maurice sits in the bleachers of Yankee Stadium, "the House that Ruth built." He follows the match closely, nothing escapes him. Go, Babe! Go! He's a real man. A winner. He looks like a fat-cheeked baby, and yet what speed! Often, he steals bases. He's funny. He's a charmer. Maurice loves him for all these reasons. If the demon of politics had not possessed him, if he had not chosen law, if he had been born American, he would have liked to become a baseball player. Not just any player. No, a great one, a famous one, like the Babe.

This evening, the Yankees are giving the Red Sox a hard time. Maurice is with a friend, a member of the Conservative Party who wants to know how he intends to get elected on May 16, 1927.

"I've asked Robert René to organize my campaign," says Maurice.

"René, the owner of the shoe store?"

"Yes. In addition to having money, the man has a lot of judgment. He gives good advice. In 1923, I made a few mistakes. The bourgeois in Trois-Rivières found me vulgar. I got the message. This time, I'm sure of beating Ludger-Philippe Mercier, Taschereau's lackey. Even the Rouges don't want him."

"Your father would be so proud to see you now, Maurice. You are so much like him."

"If I have any regrets, it is that Father died last year. He had suffered from diabetes for a long time. When he entered the Hôtel-Dieu Hospital, they amputated his leg. He was in a lot of pain… Mother also died of diabetes, almost six years ago."

Maurice takes out a flask of whisky. A quick snort. He wipes his mouth on his sleeve.

"You drink too much, Maurice. In Trois-Rivières, your benders go unnoticed. But if you want to make a name for yourself in politics…"

"Stop lecturing me. That is my only weakness. Wow! Did you see that? The Babe just had a hit. I think it's going to be a home run."

The whole stadium is on its feet. Lights are flashing on the board. Maurice is also standing. As usual, he will party late into the night and will drink heavily. Tomorrow he'll take the train back to Montreal, and then drive his car to Trois-Rivières. He has a lot to do. The election is in less than a month. Next week, he will campaign door to door. He has already prepared a long speech, which he will give on Monday.

His agenda is full. If he has allowed himself an evening out on the town, it is because he has nothing to worry about. Miss Cloutier looks after his appointments and his agenda.

∞

Louis-Alexandre Taschereau is sixty years old at the time of the 1927 election. It is the second time that he asks Quebecers to vote for the Liberal Party. He stands an excellent chance of winning. As leader of the Opposition, Arthur Sauvé does not even come close. But this time the leader of the Conservatives has an advantage. Sauvé has people capable of changing the political order. Among them are the lawyer from Trois-Rivières, Maurice Duplessis, whose star is rising, and Camillien Houde, a colourful loudmouth who likes to boast that he represents the workers of Montreal.

On May 16, the Rouges win a landslide victory. The Liberals now occupy seventy-four seats at the Legislative Assembly. The Bleus take only ten. That same evening, after hearing confirmation of his defeat, Houde announces that he will contest the election results. The Conservatives are uneasy: who has won? Who are our Members? The city of Trois-Rivières is celebrating. Maurice, the son of Nérée, has won by a hair. His victory rests on a majority of only 126 votes. Maurice Duplessis is carried in triumph along Saint-Pierre Street. It is raining. Despite the downpour, the street is teeming with people gathered to see their new MLA. There are shouts of: "Put Maurice on the hood of Lugder Madore's car! Speech! Speech!" His supporters are chanting from under their umbrellas: "He's won his spurs, *maluron, malurette!*[1] Vive Maurice!" The people celebrate and dance until late into the night.

This victory almost compensates for the Conservatives' defeat across the province. However, questions are soon being raised about the party's future: is Maurice Duplessis the Bleus's last hope? Maybe it's time for poor Arthur Sauvé to step aside for this emerging star?

Maurice hears the siren call that promises him the earth, but he is not in a hurry. First, he wants to familiarize himself with the legislature, to understand how it functions and not make mistakes. He is giving himself time. In 1928, at the opening of the session, a discreet and moderate Duplessis takes the floor to explain his party's program. The government needs to grant subsidies to the municipalities. Farmland must be protected. The Lord's Day Act must be respected.

Premier Taschereau listens to him. This young man – he will be thirty-eight next April – is impressive. He is a remarkable orator, his arguments are convincing and incisive. He wears his hair like Rudolf Valentino, is always well dressed, wears fitted jackets. He looks like an Englishman conducting serious busi-

1. Quebec folksong.

ness. Little by little, this promising young bachelor is acquiring confidence.

"I would have liked to have him on our side," muses Taschereau. During a reception at Spencer Wood, the lieutenant-governor's residence, the premier even goes so far as to introduce Duplessis to his niece. But Maurice has no intention of changing his bachelor status. Love, engagement, marriage – nothing must distract him from politics. He discovers that there is not much difference between a court of law and the Legislative Assembly. As a lawyer, he pleaded a case; as an MLA, he defends ideas. The same strategies, the same vocal effects, the same pleasure trying to charm his rivals. He is in his element. Like a fish in water, he swims in happiness.

∞

"Miss Cloutier, send a telegram congratulating Camillien Houde. He has just been elected mayor of Montreal. Add a few personal words and my best wishes."

Maurice Duplessis sees the "little guy from Sainte-Marie" as a kind of clown who makes a lot of noise. He finds him disorganized, crafty, someone who likes to play to the gallery. "A man who does not take into account his failures is a bad politician. He exposes himself to blackmail," confides Maurice to his friends.

Everyone knows that Camillien Houde, Montreal's new mayor, has his eyes on the leadership of the Conservative Party. Arthur Sauvé can no longer hold onto his position. On the lookout for a good candidate, can the Bleus resign themselves to Houde as their leader? His win in an October by-election confirms his growing popularity. Camillien, who beat Médéric Martin at Montreal's City Hall, is triumphant. As member for Sainte-Marie, he will be sitting in Quebec City. Maurice wishes him much success and, to avoid any misunderstanding, agrees to take on the sale of tickets for the big banquet in honour of Houde. On December 8, 1929, the Montreal Stadium, recently built for the baseball team, the Royals, can seat four thousand spectators. Maurice arrives by car, followed by some forty supporters, members of the Trois-Rivières delegation. In the bleachers, someone recognizes him and comes over to speak with him.

"Aren't you somewhat nervous about seeing this clown arrive at the Legislative Assembly?"

"That small fry from Sainte-Marie? No, I think he has taken on too much… Let's see how it goes," says Duplessis.

"The Conservative Party will soon be holding a leadership convention. Sauvé can't hold on. Rumour has it that he is going over to the federal side. Maurice, just think a moment. Camillien will replace Sauvé as the head of the Party, and suddenly he'll become leader of the Opposition in the House. Can't you just see Taschereau having fun with this oddball? And with us while he's at it."

"Camillien has more than one trick up his sleeve. You're wrong to look down on him. As for me, I already have too much to do in my riding. My political preoccupations can be summed up in one sentence: Trois-Rivières first, Trois-Rivières always. Since the

House only sits for two months of the year, I intend to concentrate the rest of my time in my constituency. In the meantime, my dear friend, let's go toast the Bleus!"

∞

Maurice receives his many clients and voters at his office on Hart Street. To the former, he is generous with his advice. To the latter, he promises to present their demands to the Legislative Assembly. When a good Conservative is looking for a job, Duplessis promises to find him one. People trust their MLA from Trois-Rivières, who doesn't count the hours when he's working to improve the lives of his fellow citizens. One day, Miss Cloutier asks him:

"You are free to answer or not, Mr. Duplessis, but I would like to know why I have to keep collecting all these death notices. These people don't count anymore!"

"Miss Cloutier, this list is very important, possibly even more so than the list of the living because, at the next election, there will be no more telegrams, no more cheating. My opponent will no longer be able to make the dead people vote. I'll know their names before he does!"

Duplessis leaves nothing to chance. His past mistakes have served as useful lessons. He has been in politics for almost ten years now. Nowadays, he can sense the slightest nuance. More seasoned than ever, Maurice starts off the year by steering clear of party squabbles. It is 1929. On the radio Albert Marier sings

Votre avion va-t-il au paradis? [Is your airplane taking you to heaven?], a popular song by Roméo Beaudry, one of the rare French Canadians whose songs have made the hit parade. Everyone knows the refrain that pays tribute to Charles Lindbergh in a roundabout way. Yes, the Twenties are having a beautiful ending. After the disillusionments of the Great War, the Roaring Twenties have infused everyone with new confidence.

The year 1929 is a carefree year despite the bad news that is going around. Here and there, economists are warning people: keep an eye on the stock market, stocks are fluctuating wildly. The impression of prosperity is only an illusion, be careful. While Herbert Hoover, president of the United States, talks about an era of abundance, in Canada, Mackenzie King is gearing up for the next election, which he might lose to the Conservative R.B. Bennett. In Quebec, Premier Taschereau appears secure. Who could possibly rob him of his crown?

Camillien Houde? After much hesitation, it seems that he will stand as candidate for the leadership of the Conservatives. Yes, Arthur Sauvé has finally yielded. At the upcoming convention to be held at the Château Frontenac, the only pretender to his succession will be the little guy from Sainte-Marie.

Maurice Duplessis chuckles under his breath.

∞

At the beginning of July, 1200 delegates meet in Quebec City. Camillien Houde is seated on the VIP stand and is given an ovation. The member from Trois-

Rivières is greeted just as warmly. Many would like to see Duplessis change his mind and run against the mayor of Montreal. But there is no chance of that. "If my name is put forward, I will turn down the offer," he informs the campaign organizers. The road is clear for Camillien. On July 20, 1929, the Bleus have a new leader: "He's our Mussolini!" they cry while the band plays *Vive la Canadienne*[1]. At the time, the Italian leader is basking in the glow of admiration, so this comparison is very flattering. The easygoing Camillien comes forward amidst much applause. Maurice imagines the populist Houde confronting the distinguished Taschereau at the Legislative Assembly. *It will be quite a show to see Camillien in the Opposition*, he tells himself. *When I go for the nomination, it will be as leader of the majority.*

"When I'm leader of the Conservatives, it will be to be premier," he mutters to himself.

∞

October 24, 1929 falls on a Thursday. Black Thursday. A day of disaster. The Crash. The New York Stock Exchange spins out of control. Capitalism, the cherished ideal upon which Americans have built their dream of prosperity, is crumbling. Within a few weeks, thousands of workers are jobless. Unemployment is rampant.

The province of Quebec doesn't escape the effects of the crisis. The poor are lining up for their meagre meal. Soup kitchens are set up to feed hungry families.

1. National hymn sung in Quebec before *O Canada* became popular.

It promises to be a harsh winter. How will people heat their homes? There is no money for coal or warm clothes. In Montreal, the Meurling Shelter is looking after more than seven hundred men. On Berri Street, men, women, and children in rags wait in line for food at the doors of the institute for deaf-mutes.

"It's terrible to see, Miss Cloutier."

Maurice has made a short stopover in the metropolis. Like many others, he compares the hardships suffered by the urban poor to those who are farming the land.

"The nuns give a sandwich to everyone: two slices of bread with lard, wrapped in newspaper. At least our farmers can eat from their gardens. Those who are leaving for the Saguenay and for Abitibi to homestead will have the greatest wealth there is – land to feed one's family. Just like their predecessors did before them, the ones who listened to Curé Labelle[1] and settled the Pays-d'en-Haut."[2]

Duplessis is a friend of Ernest Laforce, the Canadian National Railway agent responsible for colonization who, like himself, is convinced that a return to the land would provide jobs for the unemployed, victims of the unbridled industrial development of the Twenties. Around this time Canon Lionel Groulx, whose idea of economic nationalism is quite narrow, is also appealing to "race," that is, the French Canadians of Quebec. He reacts to the economic crisis by promot-

1. An important historical figure and a priest who promoted colonization and founded villages.
2. About 200 square kilometres around the town of Saint-Jérôme, north of Montreal.

ing a type of socio-economic nationalism. With six hundred dollars, impoverished Montrealers could rebuild their lives in the new territories that are opening up everywhere. Maurice finds himself singing the same tune. For his part, Father Albert Tessier, a friend and a powerful voice in his riding, convinces him to support a bona fide program of colonization at the Legislative Assembly:

"Quebec must be agricultural. You know it better than any other civil servant, Maurice. You have always lived in Trois-Rivières. You know how proud and independent the people are. They are to be admired for that."

"Yes, agriculture is the cornerstone of our society. Our mission is to open up new territories and settle them like our ancestors did. When I see young French Canadians going to the Université de Montréal... there's no future in that. People with bachelor's degrees, poets? We don't need that in the province."

"I'm counting on you, Maurice, and the Conservative Party, to vote for increased subsidies to fund colonization. Camillien Houde, as mayor, will be spending a lot of time in Montreal, and anyhow I have no confidence in him. You know, don't you, many still regret that you didn't take over the leadership of the Bleus last July. Perhaps one day... when you have completely recovered from your accident..."

"Ah, I'm feeling better, much better."

For Maurice, this is a bad memory he wants to forget. It happened a few months ago, on September 26. He was on his way back from a meeting in Compton. Just before arriving at Notre-Dame-du-Bon-

Conseil... he took a sharp turn too fast, and rolled his car. He woke up next day at the Hôtel-Dieu Hospital in Montreal.

"Dr. Dufresne operated on me. Do you know Joseph-Arthur? We studied together at Trois-Rivières Seminary. He does good work. All that's left is this scar."

Father Tessier is amazed by the deep scar that goes from the left eye to the back of his head. Just like a scalping.

"I almost died. I'll tell you a secret. I gave thirty dollars to Dr. Dufresne and asked him: 'Go to the Precious Blood Monastery and light some candles in honour of St. Joseph.' He's the one who saved me. If I pray to St. Joseph, it is because of Brother André, whom I knew at Collège Notre-Dame. A real saint. I inherited my devotion from him. My great hope is that he will eventually get his oratory on Mount Royal in honour of St. Joseph."

∽

Maurice Duplessis's convalescence after his car accident works to his advantage.

When Camillien Houde, the new head of the Opposition, makes his entrance into the Legislative Assembly, the enforced rest obliges Duplessis to stay away from the action. This does not, however, prevent him from following the debates to which the mayor of Montreal adds a certain flamboyance. Loud and brash, the ex-insurance salesman pays no attention to house rules. Premier Taschereau is incensed and demands his expulsion from the Assembly. Houde entertains the gallery with his antics. And yet strangely enough, the popularity of the Conservatives continues to grow.

But Camillien has a problem. He is, first and foremost, mayor of Montreal. But his position as leader of the Opposition is also time-consuming. At the St-Jean-Baptiste[1] festivities, he parades around in coat and tails. Another day, he is present at the installation of a girder for the new Du Havre Bridge, which extends De Lorimier Avenue and is scheduled to open in 1931. When Maurice returns to the Assembly, it is obvious that Houde is often absent. Duplessis becomes the de facto leader of the Opposition. During the debates, the lawyer from Trois-Rivières shines. The Liberals come to appreciate him – he is an extraordinary speaker – in stark contrast to Houde's awkward attitudes.

After four years of parliamentary work, another election is on the horizon. Maurice is not caught napping. For a long time now, he has observed what has been going on in his riding. With Miss Cloutier's help, he answers every letter. One day, he sends five dollars to the Gaieté Crocquet Club, with the words: "Your game is very interesting." His secretary asks him:

"Have you ever been to one of their tournaments?"

"No, but players are ... voters!" answers the wily Duplessis.

Thérèse Casgrain is leading the movement to obtain the vote for women. One day, she calls upon Maurice. "You must promise to support our proposal

1. June 24 – originally a holiday honouring St. John the Baptist, St-Jean-Baptiste Day eventually became officially Quebec's Fête national, sometimes known as *la St-Jean*.

and to vote for this law in the Legislative Assembly." He doesn't promise anything. He won't commit himself, but he leaves the door open. In 1931, most members feel that Quebec is not ready for such an upset of traditional values. Duplessis is one of them. To win the election, he courts other pressure groups that are more powerful. Maurice is everyone's friend, as long as no one questions the established order.

At his office on Hart Street, he works long hours so that requests for government jobs, letters of thanks to the press, all kinds of letters do not pile up. This evening, he remembers to send his condolences to Mr. Lefebvre who has just lost his mother-in-law, and his congratulations to the son of a Conservative member. "I admire your talent. What a marvellous game of bowling you played last Friday night!"

His work done, he takes a few moments to relax: a cigar and two glasses of gin. A grinding schedule. Maurice has to get up early the following day. Apparently, Taschereau intends to end the session one of these days and announce the date of the next election.

∽

In the courtyard of the LaSalle Academy in Trois-Rivières, a dense crowd is gathered about the podium. Maurice Duplessis takes the floor and launches into a diatribe against the government of Louis-Alexandre Taschereau:

"A man with no heart! His family is beholden to the big trusts."

His attacks are stark. They reach their mark.

"That old fool is a puppet. The Rouges are the servants of the monopolies. Look at what is going on with the feds. The Beauharnois scandal: Mackenzie King and his friends accepted favours. Taschereau is the same. His brother, his uncle, his son... everywhere, they reign over Quebec like monarchs. It's time to send them packing. On August 24, vote Conservative. Vote for me, Maurice Duplessis... Maurice, one of your friends."

Confident that he will be returned as member for Trois-Rivières, Maurice has his eye on power. He has already squeezed out Camillien Houde as leader of the Party. Let the mayor lead his St. Patrick's Day parades in Montreal, but when it is time to vote laws or defend a program, he simply doesn't measure up. In contrast, Duplessis is a fine parliamentarian and Premier Taschereau enjoys matching wits with him. The results of the 1931 election will determine the future of the Conservative Party.

On election day, Duplessis invites his organizers to spend the evening at his sister's house. They are gathered around the wireless radio. The evening drags on for the Conservatives, who see their candidates go down one by one. Seventy-nine Liberals crush the eleven surviving Bleus. Camillien Houde, to avoid defeat, has run in two Montreal ridings. He is defeated in both Sainte-Marie and Saint-Jacques!

And Maurice? Up to the end, he waits and he hopes. After a recount, forty-one votes give him the victory. A close call. At his headquarters in Montreal, Camillien Houde is furious. Someone advises him to contest the vote. This would oblige the eleven Conservatives just elected to tender their resignations as a group. A member of the executive committee shows up in Trois-Rivières.

"What do you think, Maurice? We have proof that the polls were rigged, too many ballots. Eight thousand dead voted in Montreal; five thousand in Quebec. If you and the ten others refuse to sit, Taschereau will have to call another election."

Polite but firm, Maurice Duplessis's *No* is categorical. His majority is much too shaky to risk fighting another battle. Resign in order to allow Camillien to return to the provincial scene? Preposterous!

"Don't rely on me to support your movement. I have work to do. I'm busy working on my own program before the session opens."

Madame Bolduc[1] is singing the R-100 song on CKAC Radio. Almost a year ago to the day, the big airship floating over Montreal was the talk of the town. Gliding over the rooftops, the dirigible with the magic number was making the children dizzy. They were running after it, twisting their necks to look up as it hung above the city. Mary Travers, alias *la mère Bolduc*, who regularly toured with her company, was inspired by the public's infatuation to write a song about the R-100, and now it is on everybody's lips.

---

1. Nicknamed La Bolduc, (1894-1941) composer/singer/musician, she performed widely and recorded ninety-four songs.

Whenever he hears the song, Maurice thinks back to the past year and its difficult moments. After the car accident in 1929, he ended up in hospital again in March 1930. An emergency. He was suffering from a hernia. And he was in much pain for several months. This time, he thought he would die, despite his sisters' encouraging words and Dr. Dufresne who came down from Montreal to look after him.

Camillien Houde's fans were on the verge of rejoicing.

"Maurice has suffered complications: stomach hemorrhages, appendicitis, peritonitis. I think he is washed up. He's going to die, for sure. Taschereau sent him a bouquet of red roses. He is as white as a sheet! He looks like a ghost."

But you can't take anything for granted. Today, bursting with health, he can look back and see himself in his white bed. And the many months he had to spend at home…

La Bolduc can be heard singing on the radio: "*Va donc mettre ton prince albert, on s'en va à Saint-Hubert…*" [Grab your coats and let's be off to Saint-Hubert.] Maurice has made great strides in the past year. Yesterday, his detractors were burying him. Today, he has never been closer to his goal: to govern the province of Quebec.

∞

The backbiting is fierce. Maurice Duplessis is accused of colluding with Taschereau ever since the premier wanted to dump Camillien Houde, who is nothing but a ranter. It's an open secret: the Liberals much prefer the member from Trois-Rivières. Even if his puns can be irritating, at least he knows how to handle a debate.

"Have you heard the rumour?" Houde asks Duplessis.

The mayor of Montreal has just travelled to Trois-Rivières to call upon his lieutenant, who is growing more and more distant.

"J. H. Dillon wants to pass a law to prevent me from contesting my defeat in the election... And to think I went ahead and blew a $69,000 deposit..." says Houde, jokingly. "Anyhow, Taschereau's gang are plotting to adopt a retroactive law that would prevent honest members like myself from contesting an election. If ever a vote is taken on the Dillon Law at the Assembly, I would like you to start a petition so that the lieutenant-governor will not be able to ratify it."

Maurice doesn't bat an eyelash. He has no intention of supporting his former leader. If Houde had worked harder at being elected in his own riding, he would not be standing there in front of him begging for allies.

And Duplessis has other things on his mind. The pot is reaching the boiling point in the province. The Liberals, feeling secure with their overwhelming majority, are not being prudent. "They're heading for disaster." Remembering his years at college when he was studying Latin, he parodies Cicero: "*Quousque tandem abtere*, Louis-Alexandre Taschereau, *patienta nostra*? [How long, Louis-Alexandre Taschereau, will you abuse our patience?] The debts are piling up and the revenues are not coming in. The Rouges, easygoing, presumptuous, are digging themselves into a hole. Convinced that they have Quebec all sewn up, they are not paying attention to their adversaries. They think that the worm of discord is in the Conservative Party's apple. Camillien's departure has reassured them.

They are wrong. Maurice Duplessis is still there.

He watches the members of the majority party and how they act. The solid front has developed cracks. The wear and tear of power has exposed rivalries. Outside the House, the Opposition is muttering quietly. A name is on people's tongues – that of Paul Gouin. The youngest son of former Premier Sir Lomer Gouin, and a lawyer, he is also the grandson of Honoré Mercier. There is talk that a group of dissatisfied Liberal members sometimes gathers at his home in Montreal.

Miss Cloutier receives a phone call from Mr. Duplessis.

"Can you get me the names of the young members of the Reform Club? And also the names of those who meet at the École sociale populaire? Apparently, young Gouin met with several of them last week."

It is 1932, and summer is almost over. The newspapers are full of the eclipse of the sun slated to take place on August 31. Maurice pokes fun at all this. An upheaval far greater than that is in the offing. Since *eclipse* is on everyone's lips, Maurice thinks that the Rouges had better be wary of the true meaning of the word.

∽

Quebec is celebrating. On March 16, 1933, Archbishop Jean-Marie Rodrigue Villeneuve is appointed cardinal. No wonder the flags are flying in the provincial capital. Many ecclesiastics from Montreal, including Msgr. Paul Bruchési, had been coveting this appointment to the Sacred College. From now on His Eminence, Cardinal Villeneuve, elector of, and advisor to, the Pope, is like a monarch. He is wearing a pallium – a white woollen stole with black crosses. Dressed in his scarlet robes, the Prince of the Church blesses the faithful. A reception is being held in his honour following the investiture. All the members of the Legislature turn out to pay him tribute.

Among them, Maurice Duplessis bends to kiss the Cardinal's ring. A practising Catholic, he goes to Mass every Wednesday morning. He believes in God, and he believes in the power of the Church. This sacred institution has always been a benefactor of the French Canadians and has acted as a bulwark for their survival. When Taschereau's Liberals passed a law on public assistance, Duplessis sided with the Church's condemnation of this law and with the State's meddling in community affairs. How dare the State take responsibility for Christian charity. It is the duty of the Church to take care of the poor, the alcoholics, the unmarried mothers, the orphans. His Eminence Cardinal Rodrigue Villeneuve likes to hear this kind of talk. He and Duplessis are on the same wavelength for many things. He finds the interim head of the Conservative Party *sympathique*.

"How do you like your new title, Mr. Duplessis?"

"My dear friend, you know that I am only replacing Camillien Houde at the Assembly. My party has not elected me. Our leadership convention will be held in a few months. Camillien doesn't stand a chance. He goes from defeat to defeat. He can no longer sit in Quebec City, and Montreal prefers Fernand Rinfret to him. But do you want my opinion? Houde still has a trick or two up his sleeve. He will come back, either as mayor of Montreal or to sit in the Assembly or go to Ottawa. He is indefatigable... like myself. You'll see, Your Eminence, in less than a year, you will be speaking to the premier of Quebec!"

∞

And what if an adversary were found to prevent Maurice Duplessis from being acclaimed leader of the Conservative Party? Camillien Houde's friends have no intention of being derailed, of not throwing a monkey wrench into the works. Their plan: convince Onésime Gagnon, a backbencher, to present himself at the leadership convention in the autumn. Who – Duplessis or Gagnon – will replace Houde?

The leadership convention is being held in Sherbrooke. Delegates from all over Quebec arrive in cars decked out in ribbons and streamers. Onésime's supporters are meeting at the New Sherbrooke Hotel. Maurice has installed his headquarters at the Magog Hotel. Primed for a fight, the member from Trois-Rivières has brought with him a group of faithful supporters whose energy is infectious. The undecided ones will soon know for whom to cast their vote.

At the convention, Duplessis rises to speak. He is calling for a program to electrify the rural areas. He wants a law to allow victims of an accident to choose their own doctor. His speech is a success. In his speech, Onésime Gagnon tries to undermine his adversary's credibility but to no avail. On October 5, 1933, Maurice Duplessis is elected leader of the Conservative Party.

He is forty-three years old and does not intend to remain long on the benches of the Opposition facing Louis-Alexandre Taschereau. The provincial election takes place in less than two years. Is he being presumptuous? Too sure of himself? Maurice has a taste for power. Working in the Opposition is clipping his wings. He wants to soar, like an eagle.

3

A Strategic Resolve

"Can you tell me why a "po-at" would bother going into politics?"

Maurice slaps his knee, a gin in one hand and a cigar smoking away in an ashtray. In his suite at the Château Frontenac, he is entertaining his friend Hortensius Béique, who is talking to him about Paul Gouin.

"You know, Maurice, maybe he's a poet, but I hear that he is recruiting people who are unhappy with the Taschereau regime."

"You don't have to spell it out for me. I already know what Lomer's son is cooking up. He should stay with his scribbling. I've read his book, *Médailles anciennes*. Have you ever heard of a guy who wants to

Maurice Duplessis during the 1920s,
at the beginning of his political career.

become premier and writes: "Your hands blackened with gunpowder, O Virgin from Verchères, wear bloodstains instead of rubies!" A premier who writes books can't be taken seriously!"

Since 1932, the rumours circulating about a third political party in Quebec have gathered momentum. A solution to alleviate poverty is being sought. Endemic poverty has destroyed a whole generation's dream of happiness. Public works programs and direct aid have proved inadequate. The worst off have even begun to hope that a war, like that of 1914, will jumpstart the economy. Where to find a job? The Saint Vincent de Paul Society is doing their best to look after needy families, handing out a meagre pittance. In winter, children are out begging in the streets. Moved by the appalling poverty in certain neighbourhoods of Montreal, pharmacist Émile Coderre, under his pen name Jean Narrache, publishes in 1932 his bestseller *Quand j'parl' tout seul* [When I'm Talking to Myself]. Yes, there are many little orphans with "dresses thin as paper." In Ottawa and Quebec City, governments remain deaf to the cries of distress and sorrow of the destitute.

In Quebec, new ways of thinking are taking root and opposition groups are springing up. The Montreal École sociale populaire denounces the excesses of capitalism and promotes corporatism. Some people are attracted by fascist ideas that are currently fashionable. In Europe, isn't Mussolini considered to be the saviour of Italy? And in Germany, has not the Nazi dictatorship found a solution to unemployment? In their search for an authoritarian and messianic leader, will people here succumb to the temptation of the Right?

Some prefer tolerance to demagogic solutions, and they are coming up with daring ideas. These people, dissatisfied with the status quo, gather around Paul Gouin, the lawyer who has been asked to lead a new progressive movement. He is joined by dissatisfied Liberals as well as the disciples of Lionel Groulx and Dr. Philippe Hamel from Quebec City. Gouin lays out a program that emphasizes co-operation and reform destined to bring about the economic and social recovery of Quebec. Among these measures is a plan for colonization, creation of a farm credit, and electrification of the rural areas. Nationalization of the electricity trusts is a project dear to Dr. Hamel. On July 28, 1934, Maurice Duplessis opens the newspaper: the program of the Action Libérale Nationale fills a whole page. He phones Paul, son of Arthur Sauvé. This member from Two Mountains is one of his most faithful lieutenants.

"Did you read the latest ravings of Gouin and his clique? Word for word, it's the program of the École sociale populaire founded by the Jesuit Papin Archambault! They trumpet all kinds of reforms: agriculture, commerce, finance, and even the elections. Absolute insanity. The world turned upside down. I've always said that intellectuals know nothing about politics."

Maurice is not worried. How could voters possibly think of supporting the Action Liberale Nationale since he, Maurice, has the best political platform? In the Assembly, his weapon is always good old common sense when he attacks the Taschereau government. The previous week, he accused the Liberals of favouring Dominion Stores because they are being given tax credits. He defended the small grocers who were being victimized by the trusts.

"I'm telling you. Paul Gouin better go take a flying leap. The real opposition is us, the Conservatives. Did you phone Bona Arsenault? I have to go to New Carlisle. I hope he's prepared a good presentation speech."

When Premier Taschereau announces the date of the election, Maurice has already been campaigning for a month. From Baie-du-Febvre to Sainte-Anne-de-Beaupré, he is criss-crossing the province. Thousands acclaim him. When he accuses the Liberal regime of bankrupting the province, or when he preaches the return to the land, Duplessis tells people what they want to hear. Cities are places of perdition, the Church is the guardian of our traditions, only the Conservatives can fight the monopolies.

Surrounded by his loyal MLAs, the leader of the Opposition uses every trick in the book. Theatrical, funny, he draws crowds. They stream into church basements or parks to hear Maurice denounce Taschereau and his deceitfulness. More than two hundred speeches. The pre-electoral tour of 1934 is a foretaste of next year's campaign. "It seems that the Action Libérale Nationale…" If by chance Duplessis hears these words, he snaps back: "The Bleus are the only opponents of the Rouges. This movement doesn't even qualify as a political party. Its members are dreamers, charlatans. There's nothing serious about them!"

As for Paul Gouin, he too is hard at work. He too attends electoral rallies. Less brilliant than Duplessis, he has nevertheless surrounded himself with a team of men who believe strongly in their ideas. Dr. Philippe Hamel, among others, is one of the more fervent proponents of bringing electricity to all of Quebec. There is no doubt in his mind that private companies such as Shawinigan Water and Power are dipping into the province's greatest natural wealth: water. The time has come to rein in this monopoly. If the Action Libérale Nationale (ALN) takes power, the Assembly will bring in a law to nationalize electricity. The idea is very attractive indeed.

Even if Duplessis publicly opposes any kind of alliance with this newly emerging political party, privately he is more prudent. There must not be three parties in the upcoming election. How to stop Gouin and his Action Libérale Nationale party from forging ahead?

At the traditional year-end banquet held in the festive red-and-gold ballroom of the Château Frontenac Hotel, the Conservatives gather around their leader. Enthusiasm has never run so high. Victory has never been so close. Maurice is more discreet. He is weighing his party's chances of success. And they are good. They would be better if the son of Lomer Gouin were not in the picture. Paul Sauvé lifts his glass to toast Maurice's health.

"Come on, Maurice, you look worried," says Sauvé, who comes over and sits down beside him.

"Did you listen to the radio broadcasts of the Action Libérale Nationale?" Maurice asks.

"On Radio-Canada? A few times… I'm not always free Sunday evenings between seven and seven-thirty.

They have been airing them for almost three months now. But I've heard about them," replies Sauvé.

"Paul, my friend, let me just say one thing: radio is a very effective weapon. We'll have to start using it. We can't allow our opponents to monopolize the airwaves. Look at Roosevelt. He's been president for the past two and a half years and you can hear him everywhere. He is a good model for our party. His idea of a "New Deal" is to put people to work on big public projects... We should introduce a similar program here."

"Maurice, Maurice..."

Hortensius Béique joins Sauvé and Duplessis.

"Tell us what the Empire State Building was like, Maurice?"

"It's not the first time I visited it. Do you know what they call it?... the Empty State Building!... because it has never been so empty. It was built just three years ago and they're having trouble renting out the offices. Unemployment in New York is worse than in Montreal. We're lucky that in Quebec we can still talk about a return to the land. Anyhow, I don't think we'll ever see a building that high in our own metropolis. No, never."

Ever since the Action Libérale Nationale started publishing its own newspaper, *La Province*, Miss Auréa Cloutier has been kept very busy. She has to record the names of the contributors, and clip articles about the subjects that often come up for discussion. This morning, Mr. Duplessis left her the telephone numbers of several Liberal MLAs. It appears that Taschereau is being contested within his own party. Fed up with the government clique, a group of activists are impatient for change. Rumour has it that the Action Libérale Nationale is trying to entice them. Maurice doesn't want to be left out.

"Tell them I want to invite them to dinner at the Château Frontenac," Maurice instructs his secretary. "I am free next week. Look at my agenda and reserve a table."

Duplessis is categorical: Paul Gouin, leader of the ALN, is a novice who knows nothing about politics. Gouin's experience is no match for his own. A member since 1927, leader of the Conservatives for two years, an accomplished debater, Duplessis knows better than anyone else the workings of the Legislative Assembly. He is the only one who can rally the Opposition and bring down the Liberals. He has trouble believing that anyone will join a brand new political group just months away from the election. Privately, however, Maurice no longer hides his exasperation. The closer it gets to election time, the more worried he becomes. His aides try to convince him that a rapprochement with certain members of the ALN is possible. "And don't neglect the Liberal backbenchers. There are always swing votes. Promise them a position in a department – secretary of the under-secretary – and they're ready to jump sides!"

Duplessis does not admit to this out loud, but he is annoyed by the whole Gouin team. Their meetings draw people. Their radio talk shows are a success. They are quality opponents. They could change the political chessboard of Quebec. Is he about to be outrun at the finish line? A wily strategist, the leader of the Conservatives analyses the choices open to him. Above all, he doesn't want to lose face. He is playing for big stakes.

He reflects: "If we were to form an alliance with the Actionnistes,[1] I would have to get rid of Gouin. I must be head of that political party. No one else."

Duplessis weighs the pros and cons of attempting a rapprochement with a man who, barely five years ago, was known only by the inner circle. Paul Gouin – collector of antique furniture, poet. That Sir Lomer Gouin's son had politics in his blood was to be expected. Now he represents a real threat to a victory of the Bleus, one that had once seemed all but sewn up. This is Duplessis's thinking in 1935. As in baseball, he feels he has lost a base to a crafty player. A disagreeable feeling. He is furious. This should not be happening. He must find a solution. Time is running out.

On January 4, 1934, Maurice Duplessis pleaded and won his last case as a lawyer. No longer the lawyer for the Shawinigan Water and Power Company, he now throws himself into politics. At his parliamentary office, Auréa Cloutier admits those who absolutely want to see the honourable member, and those who want to ask him for small favours. On the eve of the election, the list is growing. "Don't forget to vote for the Conservatives!" says Maurice Duplessis as he ushers out each guest. Soon, this magical expression is the password for landing an appointment with the leader of

1. Members of the Action Libérale Nationale.

the Bleus. Hang any scruples regarding political crony-ism. If someone is lucky enough to have a friend well placed in politics, he is sure of getting a job, a good job at a time when Montreal has almost 162,000 welfare recipients.

After a day's work that stretches from eight in the morning to six at night, Maurice goes back home to the Château Frontenac, where he lives when he is in Quebec City. Tonight he phones his friend Abel Vineberg, an old hand at provincial affairs in Quebec City for the *Gazette*. Their friendship goes back at least ten years. At the end of the week, Vineberg returns to Montreal, often with Maurice, who stays at the Ritz-Carlton Hotel.

"How are you, Abel? Tomorrow night, come and pick me up around nine. Leave me off at the Ritz. Sunday afternoon, I would like you to drive me to Trois-Rivières to my sister's. I promised to see a few voters. You can stay with us because I want to be back in Quebec City Monday morning."

Maurice's schedule is backbreaking. Every minute is taken up. During the week he manages to be in three places – Quebec, Trois-Rivières, Montreal – at three different times – the week, Saturday, and Sunday. This confirmed bachelor rarely changes his habits. There is gossip about his private life. The talk turns malicious. In Quebec City, it seems that Mrs. Flynn is his intimate friend. In Montreal, Maurice meets secretly with Mrs. Massey to whom he was introduced in Trois-Rivières. To avoid scandal, Maurice frequents married or sepa-rated women for the most part. He likes to repeat that his only mistress is politics.

On his way to Montreal, Abel Vineberg lets him in on the latest gossip circulating in the corridors of the Legislative Assembly. Premier Taschereau will probably call an election before the end of November.

"In Ottawa, Richard Bennett also has to face the Canadian electorate," adds Duplessis. "On the federal level, it's been five years since the Conservatives came to power. They have exceeded their mandate. I'm afraid that this time around, Mackenzie King is going to give them a trouncing. The Liberals have the wind in their sails... My fear is that in Quebec, Taschereau will be able to ride this wave of sympathy."

"What do you intend to do about the Action Libérale Nationale?" asks Vineberg. "Gouin is hanging on. He intends to run candidates in each riding. This is not a laughing matter..."

"I know, I know. In the old days, I could push Camillien Houde aside. But it is much more complicated with Paul Gouin."

"You'll have to find common ground with him so that ... what is the French expression?... you can cut the grass under Taschereau's feet! Otherwise, Maurice, you'll find four years in the Opposition very long!

"It's strange but I didn't see it coming. And now I have to think about creating some kind of alliance with the ALN! In the autumn, I'll see if collaboration is possible with them. By the way, Abel, are you still coming to New York next week? I'm afraid the Yankees won't make the world series. The Giants are pretty strong," says Duplessis.

"Not as strong as you, Maurice my friend. Not as strong as you."

∞

September rolls around and is very busy. Electoral promises are the order of the day. Mackenzie King and R.B. Bennett are fighting over the title of prime minister of Canada, while in Quebec everyone is waiting for Louis-Alexandre Taschereau to officially announce the date of the next election.

In his suite at the Château Frontenac, Maurice Duplessis is still hard at work perusing files he brought back from the office regarding a colonization program for the Témiscamingue region, and a document on bringing electric power to the countryside. A record is playing softly in the background. Georges Thill is singing *Qu'il est loin mon pays* [How far away is my country], an aria by Massenet. Maurice adores opera. He is a connoisseur and is proud of his collection of 78 rpm records. Many music lovers would be envious of his collection. Georges Thill is a French tenor very much in vogue whom he particularly likes. But his favourite is the good-natured, charming Enrico Caruso. The one who so often shone on the stage of the Metropolitan Opera has been dead now for fourteen years, but his unique voice is captured on phonograph recordings. In the past, in their home on Laviolette Street, Berthe and Nérée, surrounded by their four girls and Maurice, used to listen to Caruso. In the past... so very long ago!

Maurice gets up. He turns on the radio. The news is bad. Badoglio's army has invaded Ethiopia. Mussolini has extended his power beyond the borders of Italy. What is the nature of Fascism? Maurice, like everyone else, is not sure where Ethiopia is located, this African country where the ruler calls himself a *negus* (emperor). Why so much fuss about such a distant country? Things are going fairly well in the world. Adolf Hitler's name often comes up in the newspapers and on the radio. Two years ago, there was the burning of the Reichstag. And anti-Semitic laws have recently been promulgated.

It is autumn 1935, and things are heating up in Europe. Without neglecting to read the international news, Maurice is mainly preoccupied with his own interests. The Conservatives must obtain the majority in the Legislative Assembly. Tomorrow, Maurice meets his most faithful lieutenants to draw up a plan of attack.

Before going to bed, Maurice kneels down. He murmurs: *Pater noster...* the way he used to as a child when he would recite his evening prayer. He asks forgiveness from God and puts his soul into His hands. *Amen.*

∞

In the halls of parliament, the atmosphere is feverish. Duplessis is in his office with three MLAs. Ernest Laforce, the agent for colonization, enters and joins the group:

"Listen, Maurice, an alliance with Gouin's Action Libérale Nationale can't be avoided. I took a survey in all the ridings, and the grassroots in both the Liberal and Conservative parties want to reach an agreement with them."

"Listen, Ernest, I'm not a fool. I know all about the plotting and scheming that's going on. I called you here today because I want us to start talking to Gouin's men as soon as possible. It's urgent! Lucien Dansereau has a cottage at Saint-Michel-de-Wentworth. I want you to set up a meeting there with the boys from the Action. You, Hortensius, will take notes. And I want Fred Monk and Oscar Drouin from the ALN to be there. I also want a report on the meeting at the beginning of next week at the latest," demands Duplessis.

"Do you think that the victory of the Rouges in Ottawa will create problems for us?" asks Hortensius Béique, as he, Laforce, and the others rise to go. "One thing is certain, their victory will boost the Liberals in Quebec. Taschereau is in heaven!"

"I don't think our premier has entered the pearly gates quite yet. Mark my words: by the end of the year, the sky will never have been so *bleu*" [Conservative], quips Duplessis.

Maurice motions to Ernest Laforce to come and sit with him while the other MLAs go back to work. He wants news about the workers' protests in Montreal:

"It seems that the situation is even worse than last summer?" asks Duplessis.

"Things have calmed down since September," replies Laforce. "The provincial police and the RCMP have hit them hard."

"Personally, I was against the idea of cramming the unemployed into camps like Valcartier. Twenty cents a day for forestry work – even if the men are fed and housed – their living conditions are inhuman. It's not surprising that they marched all the way to

Montreal. Do you want my opinion? I think that of all the parties, the ALN is the only one that has a good social-recovery program. And that is what scares me. But we have a trump card...," says Duplessis.

"Oh yes, Maurice, what card is that?" asks Laforce.

"Money! Our electoral fund is bigger. We'll have to count on that when we negotiate an agreement with the ALN. We have the big end of the stick. In politics, money talks."

Maurice gives him a wink. Ernest salutes his leader. It's a deal. He will phone Dansereau and ask him to invite Gouin and his supporters to spend a weekend in Argenteuil County.

∞

It's Friday evening and Maurice is meeting Mrs. Massey. These romantic trysts occur according to a fixed schedule. After a week's work at the legislature, Duplessis takes the train to Montreal and gets off at Jean-Talon Station. He prefers the north end terminal to the downtown Windsor Station concourse where tourists and strollers might recognize him. His friend is awaiting him in her Outremont home for the weekend. These days, Maurice allows himself the luxury of a few love trysts. He doesn't care too much what people might say. He feels more secure. His political career is going well. And the news about the upcoming meeting with the ALN is good. Everything is turning out as he had foreseen it.

At the Dansereau chalet, the Conservatives weigh their chances of bringing about a rapprochement with the ALN before the election, which is bound to be held in less than a month. Their plan has worked! Édouard Masson, the organizer of the Bleus, tells Duplessis how the meeting went. Paul Gouin does not have bad intentions. He just wants the program of the Action Libérale Nationale to remain front and centre.

"Tell me in a few words what they call their Program of Social Recovery," asks Duplessis.

"It's simple. They compare the province to big business. They are nationalists. They want social reforms, like old-age pensions, a minimum wage, farm credit. Gouin's men are idealists."

"Ah! Now they're going too far. Here we call people like that crazy... Their program resembles Communism. It reminds me of the Bolsheviks of Russia. It's great to give to the poor but where will they find the money if they are against trusts?"

"Maurice, you've put your finger on it. The ALN doesn't have a penny. Their electoral fund is empty! We made them understand that with us, they can run candidates in most of the ridings. If they insist on going their own way, their candidates won't even have the two hundred dollars for the deposit to get on the ballot," says Masson.

"Ah! Ah! That's what I've been saying all along. Paul Gouin entered politics like a greenhorn. He would have been better off choosing religion. He might have become a good pope. But to become premier, it takes more than good ideas. It takes a nose for politics, cunning, shrewdness. Spare the rod and spoil the child," says Duplessis.

"Look at Taschereau, he's been in power since 1919. Twenty-six years. And why? Because he's backed by the big corporations. And when things get hot, he throws a few crumbs to those with the loudest voices. He knows how to silence the most impatient. You mightn't believe me, but it's Taschereau, my opponent, who has taught me the most important lessons. And now it's time for him to step aside. And not for a little guy like Gouin. No. For politicians of my calibre. Édouard, the next step is a formal meeting with the ALN. The election is on November 25. I want us to have a meeting in Montreal before the middle of the month. At the Ritz-Carlton, where I have a suite. Bring him, this famous Paul Gouin. I will make him an offer he won't be able to refuse. You'll see, my friend, by next year no one will be talking about the ALN."

∞

Montreal by night! Close to the Meurling Shelter, where the poor are crowded into dormitories, the fancy restaurants of the fashionable hotels on Sherbrooke Street cater to men sporting a Clark Gable look and women à la Jean Harlow. A bellhop at the Ritz-Carlton Hotel rushes to open a car door. The man stepping out is dressed to the nines. A dashing dandy wearing a navy blue pinstripe three-piece suit. But why is his hat so battered looking ? Even dressed up, Maurice Duplessis likes to wear slightly tired headgear. "That way, I look like a man of the people."

A lady comes up beside him. Maurice tips his hat. Always gallant, he lets the lovely stranger go ahead. The hotel employees greet the leader of the Conservative Party, a regular at the hotel.

In his room, Duplessis glances through his mail. The telephone rings. A call to say that his guests are on their way.

"Show them up!"

When he opens the door to Paul Gouin, Maurice Duplessis knows that he is about to write a page of history. This meeting is the start of a profound upheaval in Quebec politics. The handshake of these two men will determine the fortunes of a whole people.

On November 7, 1935, Gouin and Duplessis agree to join forces and present a common front against the Liberals of Louis-Alexandre Taschereau.

"My dear Mr. Gouin, your forebears are more than honourable. In fact, who among us can boast of having two premiers in their family? You descend from illustrious men, names that shine in the firmament of our nation's glory: Sir Lomer Gouin, your father, and Honoré Mercier, your grandfather."

Maurice is grandiloquent, and his praise is sincere. He can afford to elaborate on Paul Gouin's impeccable family tree because today, he, the small-town lawyer from Trois-Rivières, is the real winner.

"Let's drink a toast to the merging of our programs. Social change, exactly what we, the Conservatives, have wanted for a long time."

Duplessis can be very charming when everything is going his way, when he controls the situation. After being forced to seek an agreement with Gouin, he is happy to have finally found a solution that works to his advantage. John Bourque, the MLA from Sherbrooke, leans over and whispers a question to his leader.

"Yes, yes, John, have two forty-ounce bottles of gin sent up. Friendship makes one thirsty! And don't forget to ask for cigars."

Gouin wants to finalize the conditions of the agreement between the two parties as quickly as possible. Duplessis will be the leader. Nobody questions his ability or his self-confidence. Since the provincial election is in eighteen days, the main question is: who is the best candidate in each riding?

"Well, well," muses Duplessis, rubbing his hands. "I suggest the following arrangement: we will present thirty Conservatives, and you, sixty members of the Action Libérale Nationale. In all, ninety ridings we must win under a common banner. You can't say, Mr. Gouin, that I'm not being generous with you."

"What we really want is for our program to be adopted unanimously by your members," adds Gouin, a little nervously.

Maurice reassures him. He too is willing to fight the trusts. Electricity should be nationalized, which Ontario did back in 1906. We must spread the idea that it is time to stop the exploitation of our natural resources. Paul Gouin is satisfied.

"On November 25, when we win, I will be leader, and you will have the privilege of choosing the ministers who will form the next cabinet. Is this not a perfect arrangement?"

Duplessis embraces Gouin. The Union Nationale has just seen the light of day.

The official name of the new party uniting the Opposition has not yet been chosen but gradually, it makes its way into the political vocabulary.

As there are only ten days left before the election, and to avoid confusing the voters, it is agreed that each candidate will run under the banner of his own political party. The campaign is far from being won. Louis-Alexandre Taschereau is still hanging onto power, with a strong majority that will be difficult to beat. Nineteen years of directing the destiny of Quebec is not relinquished that easily. The Liberals are ready to take on the new political party. They are as confident as ever, because according to them, the Union Nationale saw the light of day under rushed and improvised circumstances.

4

The Art of Politics

As is his custom, Maurice Duplessis awaits the results of the provincial election at his sister Etiennette Bureau's home in Trois-Rivières. Right up to the last minute, he was shaking hands after a long speech in a church basement. He has known his riding inside out ever since the days when he travelled around it with his father. These days, he visits the towns, the villages, and the isolated concession roads by car. Sure of a personal victory in his own riding, Maurice has invited friends over for the evening. The polling stations will be closing in a few minutes. The counting of the votes is so slow that they will have to wait patiently until much later before knowing who will be the next premier of Quebec.

Maurice Duplessis, head of the Union Nationale,
with his ministers in 1936.

Maurice Duplessis, an enthusiastic fan of baseball,
throws a ball in Trois-Rivières in 1937.

Maurice smokes a cigar. His sister brings him a large gin. The atmosphere is relaxed. Edouard Masson, the organizer of the Conservatives, tells jokes. And he asks his leader if he thinks that the arrangement with Gouin will work out. Have the Bleus made a mistake? Were we wrong to throw ourselves into the arms of those we fought only a year ago?

Duplessis inhales his cigar slowly.

Is he pretending to be sure of himself? Those who know him often reproach him for his arrogance. Duplessis thinks himself better than everyone else, and he doesn't hesitate to show it.

The minutes tick by. The results are dribbling in. The announcer gives the name of the member for l'Islet: Adélard Godbout. He is a Liberal. And another name, Philippe Hamel, a friend of Paul Gouin, member of the Action Libérale Nationale. In the living room of Bonaventure Street, everyone applauds. Then, as time goes by, the numbers increase. After three gins and as many cigars, Maurice is still wide awake. He and his lieutenants count the seats: the results are encouraging. Forty-eight Rouges have been re-elected against forty-two members of the Opposition.

On the evening of November 25, 1935, Taschereau has once again been returned to power, but with a greatly diminished majority. From sixty-eight, it has fallen to six seats!

I won, Duplessis says to himself while shouting to his faithful supporters:

"The Conservatives and the Action Libérale Nationale have won!"

Paul Gouin, in his riding of l'Assomption, is speaking to his supporters. He is drinking to his victory against the Liberal MLA who sat in the Assembly for the last twenty-seven years. It was worthwhile making a few compromises. The Opposition parties had to unite forces in order to weaken Taschereau's regime. There are no regrets. At the end of the evening, Gouin telegraphs his heartfelt congratulations to his fellow traveller in Trois-Rivières and ends with these words: "We will work hand in hand." The wording is sincere and well phrased.

For his part, Maurice rejoices. He had been afraid. Without the Action Libérale Nationale, where would the Bleus be today? With the Action, he is the uncontested leader of the official Opposition. As leader, he will rise alone to face Louis-Alexandre Taschereau; in single-handed combat he will fight this tired old lion. Yes, it was well worth a few detours to achieve victory.

∽

Miss Cloutier's fingers fly over the keys of the Remington. Ding! Each time she reaches the end of a line, she pushes the lever with her finger and rolls down to the next line. She is busy typing the upcoming speeches of the member for Trois-Rivières before the opening of the new session.

The phone rings. It is Mr. Duplessis. He wants her to take out the file on the ALN and phone a friend who will confirm a rumour that has been circulating. The Liberals in Ottawa are trying to win Paul Gouin over to their side. Maurice knows that his own agreement with the Actionnistes is shaky. Some members of the ALN no longer trust him. Could it be that they are aware of his personal ambitions? Some even go so far as to want him removed as leader of the Opposition. Auréa Cloutier asks her boss if he will be in tomorrow.

"No," he answers. "I'll stay on in Montreal until Monday. In the meantime, take out the file on Liberal member Irénée Vautrin. It is very important, Miss Cloutier. Do you understand? V-A-U-T-R-I-N... Very important!"

Maurice Duplessis's greatest asset is the power he exercises over his most faithful collaborators, a handful of men who follow him blindly. Some admire him – but most of them feel that it is in their best interest to admire him. And then there are the informers, who form a class apart.

They are the privileged ones. They listen to everything that goes on in the corridors of power. They bring back what they have heard during a dinner party. They are the moles, the spies. They worm their way into everything and then come back to Duplessis's protective aura. He listens, and peppers them with questions at every turn. He has already put them to the test and put them through the mill, which is why he has such confidence in them. Their loyalty is unshakeable. And it is a guarantee of their future advancement. Maurice appreciates these men. Thanks to them, he is everywhere at once. They are his eyes, his ears. They speak on his behalf.

For a time, Duplessis fears the worst. He thinks that the merging of the two conservative parties is being threatened. "Look for some kind of confirmation that the Actionnistes are still backing us," he advises his friends. Luckily, the rumour turns out to be unfounded. At last he sees his chance in the coming session of the Legislative Assembly. After all, Gouin is a novice thrown into the political arena. Maurice can sleep in peace. Quebec City is where he will fight the battle, his own, and he has already started to mark out the territory.

∞

Abel Vineburg, correspondent for the *Gazette*, is driving to Quebec City. Relaxed and smiling, he turns to his friend:

"If I know you, Maurice, you've got something on your mind. It won't be long before you're bored sitting opposite Taschereau."

Since parliament opened on March 24, 1936, two months late, the leader of the Union Nationale seems too docile and disciplined not to be concocting some kind of political plot designed to take his adversary by surprise. Vineberg is curious about his plan. Maurice is discreet. Should he let Vineburg in on his next move? Why not? On one condition only: that Vineberg not leak the information for a few days.

"You're right, Abel, I intend to convene the Public Accounts Committee!"

Thanks to the research he has been doing tirelessly for months, Duplessis has accumulated so many proofs against the Liberals that he is now ready to mount an attack. The Public Accounts Committee, which has not sat for ten years, is a sort of tribunal that verifies the government's expenditures.

"As leader of the Opposition, I can exercise my right to convene this committee that Casgrain – a good friend, a Liberal – will preside over! The committee will be made up of thirty-six MLAs: twenty from the Liberal Party, sixteen from the Union Nationale."

Maurice admits that it is a long shot. Who knows what Louis-Alexandre Taschereau's men will do to defend themselves? Vineberg points out the growing support that this fragile government is attracting. During the winter session, didn't the Liberals talk about an old-age pension? And didn't the young and ingenious Adélard Godbout, a farmer, introduce farm policy reform?

"It is precisely to trick them, to catch them, that I'm launching into this adventure! I don't want to give them the time to win over the people with ideas that are in vogue. I have so much proof against the Rouges that I could bring them down overnight. But first I want to bring Taschereau, his family and his friends before the Committee of Public Accounts. That way, people will see that they are nothing but a band of thugs. They are so used to cheating that they won't know how to defend themselves. I can just imagine them stuttering their excuses. Being afraid. And then admitting everything."

"Is Paul Gouin aware of your intentions?" asks Vineberg.

Maurice says that they will sit side by side, even though Gouin has nothing to do with the accusations.

"I'm the lawyer. I'm the one who has initiated this attack. And believe me, Abel, I have rarely lost a case in my life!"

∞

Four days ago, the Front Populaire won the election in France. What a strange turn of events. Has the mother country turned socialist? The newspapers are brimming over with enthusiasm, but Maurice does not appreciate the rise of the Left. Luckily, Roosevelt succeeded in pulling off a master stroke with his New Deal. The American president fascinates Canadian politicians. The media salute the courage of the man who, despite a physical handicap – he had poliomyelitis when he was twenty-nine – is an amazing person. But for the moment, the leader of the Union Nationale has poured his energy into the Public Accounts Committee, which is scheduled to meet on May 7, 1936.

At the opening of the Legislative Assembly, the crowds rush in to find a seat. The best informed among them single out the main performers of this circus: Léon Casgrain, president of the Committee; Charles Lanctôt, Premier Taschereau's advisor.

Right from the start, Maurice Duplessis shows his true colours: he bares his teeth, he threatens revelations. His attacks are serious and precise. Civil servants at the Department of Colonization were lax about mailing out cheques meant for the settlers clearing land in Abitibi. The deputy ministers were paid under the table with taxpayers' money. The yellow press uncovers the skulduggery that has been going on behind the scenes for three decades now. The front page reports how Maurice Duplessis, like the true professional he is, presents his case. One by one, Premier Taschereau, his brother, his son, and most of the Liberal MLAs appear before the member from Trois-Rivières, who proclaims the virtues of honesty and probity. Everywhere the talk is about Mr. Duplessis, who has exposed the embezzlement and nepotism that gnaw at Quebec politics.

Maurice continues his efforts in order to wrap up the case. Back in his office, he asks his secretary: "Do you have Vautrin's file? Quick, I need it for tomorrow afternoon."

He is not one to deviate from his plan. Obsessed with his goal, he is going straight for the jugular. Each victory is a stage on the road to becoming premier of Quebec.

Before his defeat in the last election, Irénée Vautrin had been minister of colonization for many years. Today, sitting on the bench of the accused, he must justify the expense accounts he submitted during his mandate. With his nose buried in his files, Maurice waits a few minutes before rising. Is it true that Mr. Vautrin spent more than a thousand dollars renovating his office in Quebec? And how does he explain the bill for eleven thousand dollars for travel expenses for one year?

Duplessis bombards him with questions. Vautrin stammers his replies, red with embarrassment. The worst is yet to come. A veritable *coup de théâtre!* Maurice demands point-blank:

"Tell us about your pants, Mr. Vautrin."

Everyone in the room holds their breath. What is going on? At this point, the ex-minister makes a decision. Better to admit to everything now than to let Duplessis expound on some unfortunate detail. Just before visiting the new settlements, he had ordered breeches to be made that resembled those worn by lumberjacks.

"And so, Mr. Vautrin, you dipped into government coffers so you could have nice pants. Well, let it not be said that the Liberals go around bare-naked!"[1]

Laughter breaks out. Maurice has scored a victory. He sits down well pleased with himself. The sixteen MLAs of the Union Nationale break out into applause. They give him a standing ovation. Tomorrow, the newspapers will be full of Vautrin's pants. This embezzlement of funds is all the more unacceptable because it involves a banal pair of work pants.

With this story, Maurice Duplessis has sounded the death knell of the Taschereau regime. Paul Gouin sees the turn of events with a jaundiced eye. Certain members of the ALN are critical of Gouin's lukewarm reaction. They are taken in by Duplessis's enthusiasm and mischievousness. The Public Accounts Committee is his new stage. He manipulates his adversaries like puppets. The enemy is KO'd. He has won the fight.

Today, he emerges from this adventure stronger than ever. The Taschereau government is breathing its last. Its MLAs are being ridiculed, made fun of. Who can be trusted? The Rouges are dishonoured. A month later, the Liberal premier meets with his closest supporters to discuss how they will try to salvage their last scraps of dignity.

1. Duplessis makes a pun. *On ne pourra jamais dire que les libéraux sont des tout-nus.* "Tout-nus" means to be naked and to be stony broke.

In the ballroom of the Ritz-Carlton Hotel, the orchestra is playing Cole Porter's *Begin the Beguine*. Couples are dancing a rumba, the new dance step with its lazy South American rhythms. Seated at a table under the soft light of Tiffany lamps, Maurice Duplessis is having a drink with friends. Édouard Masson, organizer for the Union Nationale, is thinking out loud:

"I never thought Taschereau would resign so quickly! You frightened him, Maurice. You hit hard when you attacked his brother. When we found out that the money in the government's operating funds would pass through his son's hands – who just happens to be manager of a bank in Donnacona – we knew that the Liberal government didn't have a leg to stand on. But for the leader to actually withdraw from the race, that is quite a different matter!"

"You know, Édouard, I had very solid evidence. I've been collecting all kinds of information for a long time. Politics is an art. Some people will never learn how to practise it. You can throw them into the water, but they'll never learn to swim."

"Are you referring to Gouin, by any chance?" asks Édouard Masson.

Duplessis winks at his friends. He orders another bottle. Champagne, no less.

"Did I tell you about my meeting with the former head of the ALN?" he asks.

Less than a month ago, June 17 to be exact, the leader of the Union Nationale had made an appointment to meet Gouin in Montreal. Maurice arrived in the afternoon at the Windsor Hotel where Gouin was waiting with a few of his lieutenants. After Taschereau announced his resignation, Adélard Godbout, his successor, had decided to hold a provincial election on August 16. The need to renew the alliance with the Union Nationale rank and file was urgent. And this time it was out of the question for the Conservatives and the ALN to run under different banners.

For Duplessis, the time has come to do some serious housecleaning. No more concessions to please the former members of the Action Libérale Nationale. From now on, he intends to unify the two parties. And he will be at the helm of this new political force. He intends to recruit his men from among the new social classes. Farmers, blue-collar workers, and well-known personalities will be fused into a single strike force, thus solidifying support at the community level before taking their message further afield.

At the 1936 election, the Union Nationale will make its official entry under its new name, thus marking a historic turning point in the political annals of Quebec.

"I think Paul was caught short," crows Duplessis. "He saw that being in politics is not like writing little poems or buying a few pieces of old furniture."

"What exactly did he want?" asks one of his friends sitting around the table.

"The Actionnistes were sincere," says Duplessis. "Their big mistake? They are naïve. When I said we would have to ask lawyers and businessmen for money, they acted shocked. 'Never,' said Paul Gouin, 'that would be going against the premise of our electoral program.' Have you ever heard of anything so silly – a party without a healthy electoral fund?" Duplessis bursts into laughter.

The orchestra of the Ritz stops playing. A spotlight highlights the soloist, who is about to sing a tango made famous by Argentine singer Carlos Gardel, who died barely a year ago in a plane crash in Medellín, Colombia. The crowd breaks into applause on hearing the opening measures of *La Cumparsita*. Maurice and his friends continue their discussion. Édouard Masson suggests going to another bar, but Maurice is tired and wants to go to bed. He has had too much to drink. When he gets up, someone has to support him. Two of them help him to the elevator. In any case, it is very late and tomorrow morning they have to leave for Quebec City to begin drilling the troops for the coming electoral campaign.

∽

In a fit of anger, Paul Gouin and a few Actionnistes put an end to their alliance with the Union Nationale. But the majority choose to rally to Maurice Duplessis's camp. They feel that the fusion of their forces is their only chance of winning against the Liberal adversary in their respective ridings. On June 20, at the Hotel Magog in Sherbrooke, they accept the conditions laid down by Duplessis. While he brings together the more tractable ones, he leaves behind the malcontents, the undecided, the bitter, the dreamers.

Maurice emerges victorious from this new ordeal. After having ousted Camillien Houde in 1933, he has succeeded in muzzling Paul Gouin only three years later. He is undeniably a sharp politician. Cunning as a fox, he quietly has executed a strategy to eliminate those in his way. Duplessis's talent – and it's obvious he is very talented – lies in his political flair. From now on, with the exception of God, he is the only one in control, captain of a ship sailing towards victory. He has never felt so high on power.

To celebrate this tour de force, Duplessis asks that a parade be organized in the streets of Trois-Rivières. He wants to mark his triumph in a showy fashion. Cars, by the hundred, follow the leader of the Union Nationale seated in an open car. The gifted child returns to his family in the riding that his father represented for so many years. He is among voters that he knows and greets warmly.

"Bravo, Maurice!" In a single voice, the crowd cheers Nérée's son, the little boy they used to see running around everywhere. Is it true that he will soon be premier of Quebec? The region of La Mauricie swells with pride. What an honour that would be! At city hall he is received with great pomp. The city is in a celebratory mood. In a few days, he will start his campaign in Baie-du-Febvre in the riding of Yamaska. He and his lieutenants are ready to deliver the death blow to the Liberals. A few more weeks of holding meetings in Abitibi and the Gaspé, in Montreal and the Laurentians, and the Union Nationale will form the next government.

"What do you think of Adélard Godbout?" ask the more worried ones.

"I respect him. He has a solid background. He is a farmer. Compared to Gouin the poet and Taschereau the aristocrat, I prefer a farmer, someone like our own settlers, for a high position in the Quebec government."

Among the Liberal MLAs, Godbout is one of the few untouched by the scandals of the Committee of Public Accounts inquiry. It is only natural that he should replace Taschereau as head of the government. But will he win the election that has been accelerated to mid-August? Duplessis is confident. He thinks he can beat his new adversary even if the battle is tight. A new, young and dynamic team is gathering around the leader of the Liberals.

The Rouges, confident of the English vote, always start off with an advantage. Duplessis has to target his electorate: youth, farmers, nationalists. He will court each in turn. He has a lot to offer them. Is not his party independent of Ottawa? His attacks against corruption have shined up his image. More than ever, Maurice Duplessis is known as the one who exposed the political mafia. For many, he is a hero. What else must he invent in order to secure victory?

∞

Édouard Masson invites his journalist friends: Roger Maillet, Louis Dupire, and Louis Francoeur. He has a project in mind.

"Or rather, I should say it is Maurice's idea," he tells Francoeur.

"Explain what he wants."

"Maurice wants to write a little catechism for the voter. It is simple, inspired by the Catholic catechism.

Each time the word *heaven* appears, it will be replaced by 'the Union Nationale.' *Hell* automatically becomes 'the Liberal Party.' Once printed, it would be circulated around the province," says Masson.

"What a good idea. Maurice can't be beat. He understands the people, he knows what to give them," says Louis Francoeur.

"Back in 1851, Louis, Antoine Gérin-Lajoie published a political catechism which Duplessis intends using as his inspiration. He wants the questions and answers to be short, direct, and precise. And it has to be simple. Maurice told me: 'Elections are like a good Western with John Wayne. There are the good guys, and there are the bad guys.'"

"It goes without saying," continues Masson, "the Union Nationale is the only way to vote on August 16. Maurice Duplessis must be shown as the saviour of Quebec. Our own St. Michael who slays the red [Liberal] dragon. He is the one to lift us out of economic stagnation. He is the one who will give us an honest government. That will be the message of the voter's little catechism. Quick, my friends, we have work to do. But, first, I will get us some good whisky. It will cheer us on."

∞

The Civil War has been raging in Spain for a month. General Franco seems likeable enough to most Quebecers. The Catholics are well disposed towards the uprising initiated by the Caudillo. In three days' time, the rebels intend to execute a poet. But who knows anything about Federico Garcia Lorca in Quebec? It is late summer in North America. In Europe there are rumblings of war. Over there, they may be killing one another but here, it is the eve of an election that is about to shake up Quebec's political life.

Maurice rises early and goes to the polling station in his riding of Trois-Rivières. He eats with the family in his sister Étiennette's house. Later, friends will join him to await the results of the ballot. And to celebrate. Duplessis is certain that the time is ripe for his victory. He sees himself as premier of Quebec and, in his mind, he has already formed his cabinet.

Of course, gratitude is the quality par excellence in politics. The leader knows that he will have to reward his faithful militants. And not forget those who have been generous in their support. *Honni soit qui mal y pense!* [Evil unto him who evil thinks.] Who can prove that Shawinigan Water and Power paid fifty thousand dollars into the electoral fund of the Union Nationale? Was it sheer coincidence that up until two years ago Maurice Duplessis was their lawyer? Rumours. Just rumours.

"Rumours are short-lived!" says Maurice, mockingly, feeling no scruples. What counts is the final result. Victory.

In the living room, Maurice is cracking jokes. Édouard Masson, the Union Nationale organizer, is looking over the voter's catechism. They laugh and are amused by the question-and-answer format. They join the others at table. The moment has arrived to draw up the balance sheet of the election. The high point was the great rally at the De Lorimier Stadium in Montreal.

"Fifty thousand people came to hear you speak, Maurice!"

This has never happened before.

"While poor Godbout was being booed everywhere he spoke. And the Liberals, even with the support of Ernest Lapointe, Mackenzie King's lackey, are suffering. The Rouges are fading out."

People around Maurice are laughing at Paul Gouin's last-minute withdrawal. His party, the Action Libérale Nationale, is definitely dead. The fight for the election of August 16 was fought according to the wishes of the leader of the Union Nationale It is obvious, from this test of strength, that only one winner will emerge.

Maurice asks his sister to turn up the radio. The polling stations are closed. A correspondent in Montreal is describing what is going on: a giant screen is installed in front of the building of the newspaper *La Presse*. Crowds are gathered to see the results trickle in from all ninety ridings. At five minutes after eight, the suspense is over. It is official.

After thirty-nine years of Liberal government, the Union Nationale has won the election. On August 16, 1936, Maurice Duplessis, MLA for thirteen years, unelected leader of a new political party for which he was the driving force, becomes premier of Quebec.

Trois-Rivières is jubilant. At the house, Maurice is surrounded by supporters who are congratulating him, hugging him. Someone pours him another gin. The phone rings. Friends from all over offer him their best wishes. Never has an election brought such hope. A fresh wind is blowing. Has Duplessis not promised a more honest government? Seventy-six Union Nationale candidates will be sitting at the Legislative Assembly. Only fourteen Liberals will be returned to the House. The disintegration of the Taschereau regime is not to be believed.

"Maurice," says a supporter. "Do you want to hear the latest? Adélard Godbout has been defeated in l'Islet."

Duplessis draws deeply on his cigar. To find himself without an Opposition is a real break. He looks like a big shot in his three-piece suit. He is exultant, proud as punch. He makes an arrogant pout.

"Étiennette," he says to his sister, "bring the bottles that are on the kitchen counter. A victory like ours needs to be properly washed down!"

∞

Maurice Duplessis, premier of Quebec. How long he had dreamed of this moment! When he makes his entrance into the Legislative Assembly, Nérée's son takes full possession of his domain. As leader of seventy-six MLAs, he must remain calm and manage to control the most unruly ones, the rebels like former ALN member Philippe Hamel, who wants to national-ize electricity at any price – and right away. He'll have to be put in his place, that one! Maurice doesn't like to be opposed. He is the leader. Too bad if people find him bold and uncouth.

The day after the election, Dr. Hamel meets with Duplessis. He wants to obtain, as promised, the elimination of the trusts, and demands to be part of the cabinet along with Ernest Ouellet and Ernest Grégoire.

"Not so fast," answers the premier brusquely.

In the final analysis, he will choose his own men and he doesn't intend to be dictated to. His response is cutting. He has no intention of being swayed.

"Promises, promises, that's all very good. It's fine during a campaign. But afterwards, we have to look at the real priorities of the province. Nationalize electricity? I wonder if it's even necessary."

Duplessis ends up by offering Dr. Hamel the position of house leader, an honorary function that the Quebec dentist can't refuse.

Maurice's victory makes it clear to all that he is the one holding the reins of government. Have the members of the ALN who quit Paul Gouin to follow Duplessis been caught in a trap of their making? As time passes they keep going back to this burning question. Philippe Hamel can no longer control his anger. He gathers a few MLAs around him. Rumours are rife in the corridors of the legislature while René Chaloult is crying treason. A few members of the Union Nationale think of quitting.

"It doesn't seem to bother you, Maurice," observes Abel Vineberg, his friend from the *Gazette*.

"I've seen it all before. If Hamel wants to leave, let him leave as soon as possible. I need loyalty, which is the cornerstone of my electoral success. The MLA from Quebec-Centre might be able to stir up the enemy in the capital, but he doesn't have the stuff of a leader."

"Have you heard the latest about Camillien?"

Maurice has. In Montreal, Mayor Houde resigned ten days after the Union Nationale's victory.

"He never forgave me for chasing him from the party in 1933. Poor man. After threatening to go and plant bananas in South America, now he wants to mount the barricades and attack me. Don Quixote battling the windmills was a less pathetic figure than Houde!"

Camillien's personality amuses Duplessis. On every possible occasion, he attacks his former leader. Knowing that Camillien has a tendency to drink so much that he causes scandal, Duplessis recounts how recently, Camillien had to be picked up and brought back to his house on Saint-Hubert Street.

"The fellow drank I don't know how many glasses. Always the same recipe: two-thirds gin and one-third cream!"

Abel comments about the public urinals that the good mayor had installed a few years ago in Montreal. They are called *des camilliennes*.

"Lovely image for posterity," says Maurice, mockingly. "It's my turn to wonder what History will say about me when I'm gone."

Premier Maurice Duplessis visits Kenogami…

VICTOIRE
BAGOT-1938.

… and Bagot in 1938.

5

A Foretaste of Power

In 1936, the Yankees have a new hero who is as beloved as Babe Ruth. He is a tall thin guy of few words, the son of an Italian immigrant from San Francisco. Starting on the bottom rung, he climbed the ladder to become a baseball star. His name: Joe DiMaggio.

Maurice went to see him play in New York. He stood up and shouted with the crowds when big Joe hit a home run. DiMaggio is a maestro. On the field, he directs the game. His teammates only have to follow him to make short work of the adversary. In fact, Maurice likes to draw a parallel between baseball and politics. Today, he is the champion hitter. He wonders who else remains to be defeated.

Paul Gouin has returned to his former passion – antiques and the arts. Philippe Hamel wants to found a new party, the Parti National, but he is just a political lightweight. Adélard Godbout, leader of the Liberal Party, has been beaten in his own riding and no longer sits in the Legislature. As for Camillien, he is too inept to be taken seriously.

At the end of the Thirties, Maurice Duplessis reigns over Quebec almost without opposition. For many, he is a messiah, a sort of white knight, fearless and above reproach. This bachelor has taken up politics the way others take up religion. He has a vocation. To the people who love him like a father, he gives hope for a better world. Because times are hard.

Quebec has not succeeded in lifting itself out of its economic straits. Many families still require the help of the St. Vincent de Paul Society. The children who are not in school work in factories under conditions similar to those immortalized by Charles Dickens. Quebec society was founded on the values of a rural existence, and industrialization has turned Quebec upside down. Montreal does not have enough shelters to take in the jobless. The elderly keep repeating: it will take a war to give everyone work. But are parents sufficiently resigned to allow their sons to become cannon fodder?

In this apocalyptic atmosphere, the Church is the rampart against distress and despair. As soon as Maurice Duplessis becomes premier, Cardinal Rodrigue Villeneuve pays his respects. In his letter of congratulations, the prelate assures the premier of his friendship. Maurice, a practising Catholic and a fervent believer, is moved by his words. He finds His Eminence to be very agreeable.

The two men meet in the Cardinal's palace. They are made to get along together and to govern the province together. After all, is not the Union Nationale an offshoot of the Conservative Party once said to be as blue as God's kingdom?

"Hell is red [Liberal]." Maurice can still hear Msgr. Laflèche in the pulpit using these very words many, many years ago in his hometown. The monsignor was a great man and an old friend of the Duplessis family.

After thirty-nine years of Liberal rule, Quebecers have returned to the fold. Cardinal Villeneuve is aware of this. He is concerned because Taschereau has announced that he is going to give the vote to women.

"Mr. Duplessis, can you imagine for one moment what that will mean? The woman has only one duty: to stay at home, serve her husband, bring up her children. It is a great and noble mission. I can't imagine a woman getting mixed up in politics. Unfortunately, there are suffragettes like Mrs. Thérèse Casgrain. Her crusade to gain the vote for women is an American import. We are Catholic and French. I count on you, Mr. Duplessis, to put an end to these senseless demands."

Maurice reassures the Cardinal. He has no intention of giving the vote to a group that represents half the population. Why upset electoral traditions that have worked so well for him? His worries lie in a different direction.

There is great unrest among the working class, who are demanding more money and decent working conditions. Voices are being heard, particularly by union leaders who hope that the new government will lend an ear.

"What worries me, Your Eminence, is the rise of Communism."

The premier has heard that, in some companies, militants are inciting workers to defy management. Meanwhile, in the east end of Montreal, a new university of the proletariat has been founded. Pauperism, private property, collectivism – these are words that scare Duplessis. A barbaric vocabulary straight out of Russia. Indeed, Communists are redder than the red Liberals!

If ever the poor start listening to the agitators, where will it stop? Cardinal Villeneuve suggests a solution. Government should entrust the organization of work to the religious communities. For example, the Church could continue to take responsibility for all public services: hospitals, sanatoriums, schools. In this way, the unions would be effectively cut off.

"Our holy Sisters and Brothers have taken a vow of charity and obedience," points out the Cardinal. "I trust your judgment. As for the private sector, I know that you have good friends there. Is it true that you know personally the owners of the *Chicago Tribune* and the *New York Daily*?"

Maurice is proud to have as a personal friend Colonel McCormick, a finance magnate, rich as Croesus. Best of all, the colonel wants to build a mill on the North Shore that will hire five thousand workers. Thanks to the Quebec North Shore Company, a new city, Baie Comeau, will rise out of the wilds opposite the Gaspé Peninsula. It will be named after Napoléon-Alexandre Comeau, forestry guide, fishing inspector, postmaster, who was born in Îlets-Jérémie and died not far from the North Shore.

"Our natural resources are limitless," remarks Maurice to his host. "If the Americans want to come and exploit them, it'll be good business for us. They have the money, we have the manpower. You'll see, Your Eminence, in another four years you won't recognize the province."

∞

Maurice knew that his old friend, Brother André, was very sick. He had been suffering from leukemia for a long time. On January 6, 1937, it is announced on the radio that the ninety-one-year-old miracle worker has died. Maurice worries: "Did I tell him often enough that I loved him?" A memory comes back to him. After his swearing-in as premier less than a year ago in Quebec City, Brother André had come into the restaurant of the Château Frontenac. The old man, forgetting that it was a meatless Friday, had eaten steak. Misery! Such a serious sin! How to wash away this stain? Maurice had reassured his friend by promising that he would personally ask Cardinal Villeneuve for a dispensation. "Thank you," Brother André had answered. "I won't have to go to confession!"

Maurice can still see the old porter of Notre-Dame College, the first person he spoke to when he found himself alone in Montreal, far from his family. Brother André was a saintly man who had comforted the poor, the wretched, the desperate. He would dispense a few drops of St. Joseph's oil and, as if by miracle, the person would be healed. In homes all across the province, people are mourning the death of the little brother in the shabby cassock. The sorrow is sincere. People are sad. He was well loved. Brother André was part of the family. The sick would visit him hoping to be relieved. The desperate needed him because he gave them the courage to live. He gave them confidence.

As for himself, he prays directly to his patron saint, St. Joseph, the father of Jesus. Like most Quebecers of the time, Maurice has faith. Naiveté is comforting. In a precarious world, one doesn't look for questions, one stays with the answers learned in childhood. Why doubt when it is easier and simpler to let the mystery endure?

January 12, 1937 is very cold. People by the thousands are braving the weather to attend Brother André's funeral. The premier of Quebec is following the funeral procession. All wrapped up and wearing a battered hat, he bows his head. *Hail Mary. Pater noster.* He feels a part of himself has gone. Brother André is dead without having seen his dream realized. Regardless of the outcome, the Union Nationale government will find the money to erect St. Joseph's Oratory on Mount Royal. Maurice Duplessis insists on paying for part of the black marble mausoleum out of his own pocket. A final "thank you" to a man who dedicated his life to God. A man who had only one ambition: to do good on earth.

This humble man meant a lot to Duplessis. It is rare in politics to meet such a pure soul. From now on, where will he find real friends? From among the attention-seekers, those pursuing their own special agendas? Duplessis reigns over a court of toadies.

Sometimes he asks himself if that is real happiness.

∞

Miss Auréa Cloutier is staying late in the office tonight. Formerly secretary to an MLA, she is now running a premier's office, responsible for all the papers and documents.

Maurice Duplessis left her a pile of files. Once again, the famous question of electricity is dividing the party. The most impatient among them want Duplessis to pass a law nationalizing the big companies who are helping themselves generously to Quebec's natural resources. Maurice detests being pushed. Hotheads who can't see beyond the tip of their noses! Braggarts who think that public affairs are managed like the budget of a rich family. At the same time, Maurice knows that he owes his victory to his friends. That it is best not to rush matters. He gives his secretary a list of the people he wants her to contact while he is away on holiday. Duplessis hasn't taken a day off in six years.

"I'm off to Bermuda. I'll be back before parliament opens. Keep me informed about the rumours that are circulating about me, from the stupidest to the most serious. When the cat is gone, the mice will play. When I return, I don't want to see a bunch of birdbrains who think they are Mussolini! Keep an eye on Oscar Drouin. I have my people watching him, but I know that you, Miss Cloutier, have something the others don't have – feminine intuition. The sixth sense doesn't lie!"

Maurice loves to tease his secretary. When they're together, they look like an old couple cemented by a mixture of suspicion and complicity. They size each other up. They know each other's limits. Auréa Cloutier looks at her boss as if to say: Enough, you've loaded me up enough. My hands are full.

This spinster is by far the toughest woman he knows.

It is the beginning of 1937. Duplessis is collecting ammunition for his new role as premier. The atmosphere is tense. Some think that the leader of the Union Nationale won't complete his four-year mandate. Political stability, in Canada and abroad, is deteriorating rapidly. America is still enjoying the spurt of economic activity that revived Roosevelt's fortunes and got him re-elected three months ago.

Quebec is not touched by the hysteria sweeping through entire nations and sweeping through Europe. The cult of leader is widespread as if to compensate people for life's difficulties. Hitler in Germany, Stalin in Russia, Mussolini in Italy, Franco in Spain. Like lemmings rushing toward the cliff, people seem blinded by a vindictive and dominating father, resigned to distress and destruction. Twenty years after the Great War, will another generation of men and women be sacrificed?

Personal conflicts within the Union Nationale are dwarfed by the storm brewing outside Canadian borders. Back from Bermuda, Maurice realizes that he was right to suspect certain MLAs. Oscar Drouin and Dr. Philippe Hamel, too dangerous in their determination to nationalize electricity, are thrown out of the party. To please the population, the premier announces a cut in rates and suggests nationalizing a few companies – the less important ones – those who do not contribute directly to the electoral fund.

Duplessis reacts to opinion like a conjurer. He gives with one hand what he takes with the other. Yet he is prudent, knowing how little experience he has at being head of a government. This first mandate is a dress rehearsal for the second mandate which will be much more illustrious. His first steps are awkward. He works hard at being premier. He looks for allies and finds them among the thinking elites, those who served the Taschereau regime.

The Catholic Church, represented with great pomp by Cardinal Rodrigue Villeneuve, is devoted to him. Maurice Duplessis often meets with His Eminence. They share the same concern: Communism is a real social ill, an endemic disease that has to be eradicated. What medicine will wipe it out? In Montreal, a few months earlier, Msgr. Gauthier was able to mobilize an impressive number of anti-Communist protesters. In Quebec City, twenty thousand loyal supporters came to hear Cardinal Villeneuve's diatribe against the Communist devils. Maurice Duplessis stood up and gave a rousing speech at this gathering:

"Dear friends, I promise to banish Russian films from our screens. They are only propaganda, bad ideas that come from elsewhere."

The crowd applauds. What would become of Quebec if the Communists took power at the next election? It is unimaginable. No more bosses, no more work. Fortunately, Duplessis and Cardinal Villeneuve are on the alert. Standing side by side on the stage of the Quebec Coliseum, they have a common project, an enemy to fight. Ah! These evil Reds, they will send them back to where they belong – to hell!

"The labour unions who are shunning the Catholic proposal to reach a truce between employers and employees must be abolished," says Cardinal Villeneuve in a firm voice. "This is not the moment to have strikes, or to fight for better working conditions. What next! Salary increases, reduced working hours! It has already been so difficult to come out of this economic slump. Our people should be happy to earn their bread with dignity wherever they can."

Maurice Duplessis is satisfied with the prelate's support. After all, the people who advance these crazy political ideas are atheists. Moreover, it is not only in Quebec that Communism poses a threat. In Spain, according to the propaganda that is filtering back into Canada, the Reds are torturing priests. The emulators of Karl Marx will not find favour in Quebec. Those who wish to spread his doctrine are in a minority in isolated pockets. They have their own newspaper, *La Clarté*, which circulates among the militants.

These fanatics irritate Duplessis. Protests against capitalism have to be nipped in the bud. But how? Before the start of the next session, the premier calls a meeting of his closest supporters. He tells them he is creating a law that would give the public prosecutor of the province – himself – the right to close any establishment that produces tracts, documents, or newspapers emanating from these crazy Communists! His friends applaud his courage.

"Mr. Duplessis, you are right in assuming your responsibilities and taking things into your own hands. We have reached the point when a handful of agitators could foment trouble among the poor workers in the east end of Montreal."

The leader of the Union Nationale is proud of his coup. On March 17, 1937, after a long speech highlighting the moral values of Quebec, most of the MLAs vote for what is now referred to as the Padlock Law. It will be used against union leaders.

The witch hunt is about to begin. Once this law is proclaimed, the Communists become the "bad guys" in a sort of western, with its comical, but mostly dramatic, twists. Where is the Left? Here, in the offices of *La Clarté*. The provincial police have orders to padlock this den of revolutionaries. People breathe a sigh of relief. Premier Duplessis is keeping an eye on the wrongdoers. Few dare to contest his ideas. The *"chef"*[1] has spoken. There is no opposition to his discretionary powers.

But what constitutes Communism in Quebec in 1937? A few hundred sympathizers who are critical of a collapsing capitalist order and who believe in utopia. Nothing very serious. But among these militants, there is a group of men whose influence he has always feared: the intellectuals.

---

1. Duplessis's nickname, meaning "chief."

They are his real enemies. He ridicules them. He demonizes them and always ends up making a nasty remark: "Intellectuals? Nothing but *pianer* players!"

Maurice Duplessis has found another way to prevent the voters from east-end Montreal from ever being tempted by leftist ideas. He appoints one of them to the position of labour minister, a nobody from their neighbourhood: William Tremblay. At meetings, this colourful personality snaps his suspenders and proudly claims: "I'm a worker!" Duplessis congratulates himself for having chosen a man who resembles Camillien Houde.

But what is happening to the ex-mayor of Montreal, the former head of the Conservative Party, Maurice's ex-leader? Someone close to Duplessis confides that after Houde's defeat in December 1936, he was so discouraged that he decided to go into exile in Venezuela. So the rumour was true: he wants to buy a plantation and export bananas to Canada.

"Another one of his whims! I bet he'll soon be home. And not for bananas or peanuts, but for politics. When I see Tremblay, I think of Houde. Quebecers like this kind of politician who reminds them of the good ol' days and the kind of campaigns my father used to run in Trois-Rivières. By the way, William Tremblay talked to me about a pretty interesting project that could give people work. I have the impression that this time my government will finally be appreciated for the right reasons."

∽

Brother Marie-Victorin is a botanist of some repute. His young naturalists circle attracts young people with an interest in botany. His book on the Laurentian flora is selling well. In October 1936, the botanist asks to meet the labour minister to present a proposal for a major project, a large undertaking that would give work to many of the unemployed. It would resemble the public works projects that Roosevelt set in motion to counter the effects of the 1929 Crash.

Tremblay, the labour minister, is drunk when he receives Brother Marie-Victorin in his office. He is vulgar and uncouth in his manner. The Brother, feeling somewhat dismayed, nevertheless persists. He won't give up even if he has to petition Duplessis for a grant. Money is what the brother wants – money.

"Sixty thousand dollars!"

To everyone's surprise, Maurice Duplessis is interested. He feels that the government's coffers are sufficiently well filled to launch into such an adventure.

"A botanical garden in Montreal? In the east end, in the Maisonneuve neighbourhood, where there is so much unemployment? A project after my own heart."

By spring of 1937, dozens of trucks loaded with rich black earth rumble along Sherbrooke Street towards Pie IX Boulevard. Inside the perimeter of the garden, workers transform themselves into horticulturists. They plant trees, North American rose bushes, blue spruce. In the urban greyness, a green oasis gradually takes shape. A virtual miracle. Brother Marie-Victorin thanks the donors, the Union Nationale and its leader. He will be eternally grateful to Duplessis for allowing him to make his dream come true, but the friendship between the botanist and the premier will always remain distant and polite. The two live in parallel worlds that are irreconcilable. Maurice, who loves making fun of pedantic people, admires this scientist who is not like the others, this intellectual who smells of earth, who is not afraid of digging in the dirt so that he can ferret out the secrets of Quebec's flora. Brother Marie-Victorin is a bit like a peasant, only more educated. He is lucky.

While a neighbourhood of the big city is undergoing transformation, Maurice Duplessis foresees other social changes. He has now been in power for a year. He has started a fight with Ottawa. He wants Quebec to receive its fair share of revenues from the federal government. His Ontario counterpart, Mitchell Hepburn, supports his endeavour. During their meetings in Montreal and Toronto, they agree to join forces against the Ottawa Liberals. But Mackenzie King's government is not ready to listen to their complaints about the sharing of fiscal powers. So what if Duplessis wants more control over public finances!

On Parliament Hill, people are very wary of him. There is absolutely no question of giving too much latitude to the leader of the Union Nationale despite his ongoing popularity. Duplessis calls his lieutenants together to announce that he will remain firm with Mackenzie King and his lackeys, especially Ernest Lapointe, who is talking about abolishing the Padlock Law. The fight has only just started.

This marks a sharp turn in Duplessis's career. He has become the autonomist premier invested with an exceptional mission: save Quebec from the claws of the centralizing government in Ottawa.

On the stage of the Monument National Theatre, Gratien Gélinas,[1] cast as Fridolin,[2] has the audience in stitches. With his Canadiens hockey sweater and his cheeky cap, he looks like a real scallywag who thumbs his nose at everything. An impertinent, bold little Quebecer. His weapon? A slingshot. His enemies? Fools.

In 1938, *Fridolinons!* is a very popular show that attracts audiences of all ages. It is a sign of the times. This hero is beloved because he dares to say out loud what people are thinking. He comments on the political scene and his monologues are political attacks. Crowds are lining up at the box office on St. Lawrence Boulevard. Extra performances are advertised on the marquee.

Like he is every Friday night, Maurice is at the Ritz-Carlton Hotel. He has bad habits and his health is starting to concern him. Recently, his doctor warned him: "Be careful. Your parents died of diabetes. Remember how we had to amputate your father's leg a few months before he died? That could happen to you."

Maurice disregards his warning and continues to drink heavily. On his own, he can empty a forty-ounce bottle of gin, and he smokes one cigar after another. At this rate, some people think he won't finish his first term as premier. Abel Vineberg, after handing in his

1. Playwright, actor, director – a towering figure in Quebec theatre.
2. A teenager pretending to be naive who comments on the social mores of the day.

column to the *Gazette*, joins him. The two friends discuss politics and the social climate, which has deteriorated over the past year. The strike in the nine factories of Dominion Textile has undermined the power of management, where Duplessis's sympathies lie.

"I had to pass the Fair Wage Act. I didn't do it willingly. It was the only way to keep the workers quiet."

"You won't regret it, Maurice. Firing a worker only to rehire him again in a lower-paid job couldn't go on. Your law threw a monkey wrench into the works. Today, it is more difficult for the unions to call a strike. Isn't that what you want?"

"I don't like the unions. There are too many cranks in those associations. I know that some newspapers – particularly in the English press, my dear Abel – are branding me a Fascist. A silly accusation. It's not for nothing that I am in politics, I have my own objectives. I'm not interested in tinkering with the school system or welfare. But based on the recommendation of the Action Libérale Nationale, I did pass a bill to support needy mothers. I intend to increase farm credit and to repatriate old-age pensions from Ottawa. Quebec is like a big family, rowdy but easygoing, protected by Church and State. I resent the unions trying to impose a system that doesn't suit our society. I'm the boss, after all! I'm the one the people voted for, with a clear majority."

Duplessis has trouble getting up. He sits down again abruptly. The alcohol has gone to his head. What he won't admit is that everything is going badly, and that he is having trouble controlling his life. Recently, someone told him that the transport minister, François Leduc, could cause a scandal. Should he force his resignation? That is probably the only solution to prevent the party from suffering an internal crisis. Abel Vinebeg is aware of the Leduc affair. In the corridors of the Legislative Assembly, tongues have been wagging. The press is fanning the flames of gossip.

"I can't tell you any more, Abel. It's not because I'm premier that I'm the best informed. But I can tell you that I have a file full of complaints against Leduc. If I let him continue, he might become dangerous. I have made an appointment to see him in a few days. We'll meet at the Château Frontenac. I intend to tell him to resign and I'll drop the accusations. Because, in the end, Leduc is a very intelligent man. He has talent, he's an engineer. I don't have many like him among my ministers. Guys like William Tremblay who make everyone laugh, they're easy to recruit. But someone like Leduc, I'm really sorry to have to show him the door."

Vineberg cautions Duplessis: if Leduc refuses to go, what will he do? There are few solutions open to the leader of the Union Nationale.

"I'll go as far as asking for the resignation of my entire cabinet. After the official ceremony at the lieutenant-governor's, all my ministers, except Leduc, will be sworn in again."

"Would you go that far to expel a minister? It's never happened before in the history of our country."

"Listen to me. At the moment, I'm the one making history in Quebec. And if my name is remembered later on, it will be because I dared to do what others never did!"

∞

"Happy New Year!" The year 1939 is ushered in with confetti and streamers. The guests raise their glasses and toast prosperity, happiness, and "paradise until the end of our days," adds Duplessis.

Maurice likes to use this ready-made formula. Everyone laughs, it's friendly even if some people reproach the premier for his populist and sometimes rather gauche manners. He likes to exaggerate. He loves worn-out jokes. But he does have an irresistible way of telling them. In a party, like tonight's New Year's Eve *reveillon*,[1] Maurice enjoys entertaining his family and his friends. He tells how François Leduc was demoted from his job as minister of transport. Maurice ended up using the strategy that he had outlined to Abel Vineberg. The whole cabinet had resigned and been sworn in the following day minus the trouble-maker! A body blow, a clever plot that Duplessis still has to justify. In public, he takes the opportunity to make everyone laugh with his puns and his word games. He trots out his old jokes made at the expense of his opponents, like the scathing remark against the clerk of the Executive Council.

"I gave a cigar to Morissette and I told him to smoke it so that I could have the pleasure of seeing something come out of his head!"

Duplessis is an actor. He loves to mime the reactions of others. Nothing pleases him more than to pin down the person he is speaking to. He is convinced

1. A festive meal celebrated on Christmas Eve or New Year's Eve.

that he is smarter than anybody else. He speaks with a loud voice. He has a loud laugh. He is not boring at a party. And yet, these celebrations are overshadowed by nostalgia, as if the atmosphere is tinged with sadness. The conflicts in Europe are still going on. Why didn't the Munich Agreement of September 1938 put an end to the threat of Hitler's annexations?

Maurice, who follows the news avidly, claims that the prime minister of Canada, Mackenzie King, will soon be faced with difficult decisions. In Ontario, two hundred pilots are waiting at Rockcliffe Airport to lift off for Europe. The world is sleeping on a volcano. While France and England have not yet fully grasped the magnitude of the Nazi nightmare, China and Japan are tearing each other apart. When the war finally does break out, it will be on a world scale.

And when England declares war on Germany for the second time in less than twenty years, Canada will have to join under the British flag. Painful memories of the draft resurface. There is fear everywhere. Almost every family has a son of fighting age who could run the risk of dying there in the trenches, like the thousands of French soldiers who perished in Verdun.

Duplessis has no children of his own. But he knows that his friends have good reason to be worried. And he knows that among his deputies there are men who could be called up to arms, like Paul Sauvé. There is speculation that Sauvé might succeed him as head of the party.

As premier of Quebec, Duplessis is not very free to act in the event of a national political crisis. He will have to follow Ottawa's directives. Something has been bothering him for the last few days. *Later*, he thinks, *maybe next month I'll meet with my closest collaborators. And we'll discuss it. Until then, I can relax.*

Maurice asks for silence. He has an important piece of news. It is official: King George VI and his wife, Queen Elizabeth, will be visiting Canada in the spring. Their itinerary will include visits to Quebec City and Montreal. And yes, big burly Camillien Houde, re-elected mayor of Montreal, will have the honour of receiving the royal couple. In Quebec City, the celebrations promise to be sumptuous. Maurice is thrilled: "We'll bring out the Union Jack. And to please Cardinal Villeneuve, the Sacred Heart flag." As loyal subjects of His Majesty, Canadians will render homage to their King. And Quebecers don't want to make a sorry showing. Duplessis will see to it that they don't.

Ah, yes, 1939 will be a beautiful year.

As Étiennette Bureau passes around plates piled high with doughnuts and biscuits, her guests try to be hopeful. "Put on some music, Maurice," she says to her brother. "Why not Ray Ventura's *Qu'est-ce qu'on attend pour être heureux?* [What are we waiting for to be happy?] It's a joyful tune, and the young people will be able to dance the swing."

6

Defeated... Now What?

A decision has been made. Maurice Duplessis is convinced he has made the right choice. He could remain in power for at least another two years, but he will call an early election – for October 25, 1939.

Most of his MLAs don't share his confidence. They were hoping to stay the full four years. Duplessis tries to convince them that the Union Nationale has to secure its position on the Canadian political scene. Paul Sauvé is among those who support the leader's decision.

"The province is with us, Maurice. We have won all five by-elections since 1936 and Godbout's Liberals are in disarray. Your strategy is the best. Since 1917, people have blamed conscription on the Conservative

In 1939, Maurice Duplessis poses with leading dignitaries during the visit of King George VI.

Party – which is where our roots are. This time, Quebecers are bound to understand that it's the Liberals in Ottawa who want to send their children into combat in Europe."

"France and England declared war on Germany on September 3," says Maurice. "And in the last three weeks, things have moved very fast. We must make it clear in our speeches that Mackenzie King is taking advantage of the situation to curb our power. His new minister of defence controls the loans to the provinces. We have no more money! All our projects have failed. A few days ago, I asked the Bank of Canada for a loan of forty million dollars. They refused. The provincial election will be a good opportunity to defend ourselves against the federals. Listen to my slogan, Paul. I intend using it in my campaign: Co-operation always, assimilation never."

"Quebecers aren't crazy," says Paul Sauvé. "The War Measures Act that Mackenzie King has just passed violates their individual rights. This is very serious, and it will remind them of the excesses committed during the First World War when Borden allowed the RCMP to force young men out of hiding in their homes. Everyone remembers the roundups of young men and how conscientious objectors were thrown into prison. We're not there yet, but the memory is still very much alive."

"There was a lot of talk against your Padlock Law," he continues, "but Ottawa doesn't hesitate to censor radio broadcasts and newspapers when it suits them. It would be good to bring this up during the campaign. Godbout will have a hard time finding arguments against us. I bet we'll win the October election, Maurice, with our biggest majority. We have what it takes to succeed."

Neither Duplessis nor Paul Sauvé believes that Canada is threatened by Hitler. The two men are amused to see Mackenzie King behave like the defender of Western civilization against the bad Germans when, only two years ago, he paid a visit to Adolf Hitler.

"Did he consult his fortune teller? I'm sure she's discovered a new enemy in the crystal ball," says Duplessis, ironically, taking every opportunity to poke fun at the esoteric beliefs of his federal counterpart. "What really bothers me," he adds, "is seeing us totally devoted to the British Crown." Maurice corrects himself. He doesn't need Paul Sauvé to remind him that in May he was very pleased to receive King George VI and Queen Elizabeth. "I even gave a long speech in English. With Cardinal Villeneuve by my side, the occasion did not lack for pomp and ceremony."

But at least he can claim to be less carried away than Camillien Houde, who asked Montrealers to wave flags as if they were receiving the royal couple in their homes.

Camillien hasn't changed. He goes, he comes, and he is always the same performer, exuberant, tireless. "I wouldn't be surprised," concludes Duplessis, "if our good mayor of Montreal ran into problems within the next few months. He is an individualist. He doesn't have the stuff of a leader. He never learned how to control his troops the way I do."

"I know there are people out there who are not pleased because I called an early election" says

Maurice. "Maybe they will criticize me if they are defeated. I know I am taking a chance. Godbout is not as insignificant as he might seem. I certainly respect him as an adversary. And he has the support of the big Liberal machine represented by Ernest Lapointe, minister of justice in Ottawa. I'm keeping my eyes on that one. If they succeed in funneling money into the provincial campaign, we'll have a serious opponent on our hands."

The 1939 October campaign promises to be a difficult one. The francophone ministers of Mackenzie King's government have no intention of allowing the leader of the Union Nationale to manipulate public opinion as he wishes. They know he is cunning, a clever strategist. To win against him, you have to take the offensive immediately. Conscription has become the main issue of this election.

England is busy arming against Germany, and Canada is caught up in a vortex from which the country will not emerge unscathed. Blood will be spilled and young people sacrificed in the name of freedom. People are saying that there won't be enough volunteers to go around, that conscripts will have to be called upon, men who don't want to serve.

Ernest Lapointe is the keenest on seeing Duplessis defeated. But how to engineer it? He needs a good idea. Along with other members of Parliament, he threatens to resign if Ottawa passes a law on conscription. This is a real coup and a real boost for Adélard Godbout's Liberals. Now they can tack onto their program the promise that enlistment will not be mandatory as long as people vote for the Rouges.

Duplessis is shocked. Will Quebecers believe this lie? He rounds up his men.

"Ernest Lapointe's strategy is a blow against the Union Nationale. By threatening to quit the government, the federal francophone MPs will isolate the province from the English majority. How will our party look? We don't have much power, we don't sit in Ottawa. We have only one hope left. Maybe voters will see through the schemes of these hypocrites who are pretending to save our youth."

Paul Sauvé points out that Godbout and his men are about to launch a series of radio talks that will allow them to reach thousands of voters. Shouldn't the Unionistes also invade the airwaves?

"Never!"

Duplessis's answer is categorical. He is afraid that his speeches will be censored by his opponents in the federal camp who control the contents of radio programs.

"We are at war. It would be an ideal pretext to stop the truth from coming out. We will campaign as usual in the small parish halls, and we'll go from door to door. We'll organize large gatherings in the cities. In Montreal, we'll fill the De Lorimier Stadium like we did three years ago. In a few days, I'm leaving for the Gaspé. I phoned Bona Arsenault so that he can start warming up the crowds. I'll go to the Eastern Townships, to Abitibi, I'll go as far as Sapin Croche Lake if I have to. The Liberals will not have it easy. I haven't said my last word yet. On October 25, I will again be premier of Quebec."

∞

"Maurice, have you heard the latest? Camillien Houde is running as an Independent in the Sainte-Marie riding."

Abel Vineberg confirms the rumour. The news couldn't be worse. The mayor's candidacy is creating discord. Maurice discovers that he can no longer count on the support of the working-class neighbourhoods. And that he will have to redouble his efforts not to find himself head of the Opposition. Slogans against him have been multiplying among the Liberals. Vote for Duplessis and leave the province defenceless.

Under his calm exterior, Adélard Godbout seems determined to win. No one knew he packed so much energy and determination. His three years outside the Legislature have given him time to develop a progressive electoral program. Godbout's projects include nationalizing electricity and giving women the vote, projects that he wants to see implemented and which the premier will have to deal with. By resisting radio as an effective medium to reach voters, Duplessis is failing to measure up to his opponent. His friends are worried.

"Did you see Maurice recently at the Trois-Rivières meeting?" asks Édouard Asselin, an important colleague of Duplessis's and a lawyer from Shawinigan. "It was pitiful. He was drunk, completely drunk, and he wasn't talking straight. He mixed up conscription and participation in the war. Nobody, either in Quebec or Canada, wants to re-examine the question why we are fighting Nazi Germany. Maurice didn't act like the responsible head of a government engaged in a conflict whose end is not in sight."

"There was much talk about how he ended his speech," adds Édouard Asselin.

Asselin recounts how Maurice, in a great theatrical gesture, held up the tricolour banner on which were embroidered the words: *Je me souviens.*[1]

"We wondered how far he would go. Paul Sauvé whispered to me: it's the champagne and the gin that have gone to his head. Let's end the meeting and take him home."

Asselin is sure of it. Maurice Duplessis is about to bring defeat upon the Union Nationale.

"Even if he chalked up several successes during his first mandate, like the Botanical Gardens or the fight against certain trusts, people continue to criticize him for the Padlock Law. His enemies, who include a good number of intellectuals, carry grudges. His weak point is his contempt for those who don't think like him. Duplessis is vulnerable. The election on October 25, 1939 will teach him a lesson. I only hope that he can draw the right conclusions."

Like Asselin, many Union Nationale members realize that the fight will not be as simple as their leader had told them when he decided to call an early election. But there are those whose confidence in their leader is unshakeable. A few days before the vote, at the De Lorimier Stadium, Montrealers welcomed the nationalist leader as their hero.

"Thanks to my government, we were able to protect our laws that defend Catholicism, the French language, education, the settlement of the North. In

1. Quebec's motto. In translation, it means "I remember."

Ottawa, we are only a minority. To vote for the Union Nationale is to ensure our survival as a people and as a nation."

Duplessis is all puffed up. But he is dreaming. During his electoral rounds, he goes to Yamachiche, his father Nérée's old fiefdom, where he is received politely but without great enthusiasm. Then he returns to his hometown for a last rally. "As usual, I will await the results in Trois-Rivières at my sister's," he says to his closest allies. "I will have champagne and cigars on hand. I will expect you around nine."

∽

Montreal elected only Liberals, with the exception of one Independent, Camillien Houde. The province is Rouge, with a few Bleu spots here and there. Maurice hung on to his seat with less than two thousand votes.

On October 25, 1939, Adélard Godbout becomes premier of Quebec. At the head of sixty-nine Liberal MLAs, he is enjoying the victory that his backers had predicted. Maurice is wiped out. Ironic, he recalls: "I had asked Miss Cloutier to place a three-thousand-dollar bet on the Union Nationale to give us ballast. When the Ottawa machine gets involved in what is not its business, what can you expect? I'm happy that at least I was able to get fourteen MLAs elected."

Duplessis has a hard time seeing himself back in the Opposition. In reality, he is balking at the idea, not only out of pride but also because he feels he won't have sufficient time to complete the great projects he had envisioned. A friend reassures him: Godbout will probably have a very rocky mandate. How will he set himself apart from Ottawa if Mackenzie King passes a law on conscription? The day isn't far off when the Rouges will have to bite the bullet. The war has only just started. Soon soldiers will be leaving. What do people have against Godbout? His lack of leadership, his secret connection with his federal cousins? At least Duplessis is lucky enough not to be compromised by this imbroglio.

"Be patient, Maurice, you'll be back even stronger in four years," his friends tell him. But patience is not one of his virtues. He has aged and his health is less than perfect. He is taking the defeat personally. And he is partly right.

"You made some pretty serious mistakes," his closest colleagues remind him. "If you had spoken on the radio, you could have explained where you stood with regard to the war in Europe."

Others are more direct: "You drink too much. If you want to be in politics, you'll have to put the bottle aside." Maurice doesn't like to hear these criticisms. But he accepts them reluctantly. They are valuable lessons. But in 1939, there are more serious reasons underlying the Union Nationale's difficulties. Duplessis's team is not aware of them on election night. Right now it is time to heal the wounds, and not to analyse. After a few days' rest, they will assess the situation. Quebec is undergoing a transformation and entering the modern age. *Where did the voters go?* wonders Duplessis. His support used to be in the countryside. Now, the majority of people have moved into the city, and they want nothing more to do with his party.

"How can we appeal to them in the next four years since the trend towards urbanization is irreversible?" he asks one of his strategists.

The day after his defeat, despite his fatigue, Maurice considers himself already embarked on an electoral campaign. He is a good loser and encourages his defeated supporters and MLAs. He won't abandon them, he says. If he can help them, he will.

At the beginning of November, he receives a confidential letter that warms his heart. Cardinal Rodrigue Villeneuve assures him of his friendship. Why is this letter so important to him? The prelate and the leader of the Union Nationale need each other. Quebec society functions in such a way that political power rests upon the power of the Catholic Church. *When I am re-elected, Cardinal Villeneuve's support will be very precious. I'll be able to count on his trust in me*, thinks Duplessis.

But in the meantime, he has to take care of the grumbling party members. The unhappiest among them, those who have benefitted most from the system of political patronage, would like the Union Nationale to fuse with the federal Conservative Party.

"Never!" Maurice's answer is clear and unequivocal. He is committed to the independence of the party he created four years ago. For one moment the worst is feared, a crisis, dissent. Onésime Gagnon's name comes up as a possible leader. But it's unthinkable! Duplessis is determined to nip in the bud the slightest attempt at contesting his leadership. To this end, he continues to surround himself with committed militants in whom he has absolute confidence. One day, someone introduces him to a businessman who has made a fortune with Zellers. "Gérald Martineau, he's royal Bleu! He wants to work for us."

A firm handshake follows. It is understood that the newcomer will occupy an administrative position in the party. Being treasurer is a role that suits Martineau. Duplessis recognizes a natural ally when he sees one. These are his troops, the strongest among them, who are moving up through the ranks. Their advice is obviously useful to him, but he is the one who makes the ultimate decisions. It is time to reorganize the party. He divides his troops in order to better reign over them. A tried and true Machiavellian principle that still works.

Martineau becomes one of Duplessis's inner circle right away. He joins him at the Château Frontenac in his suite that smells of Havana tobacco. There is a bottle of gin on the table. Maurice is scribbling down the names of MLAs whom he trusts. Anyone who opposes him should be given the door! In these difficult times, he doesn't give a second chance to any of his detractors, and he wants that understood once and for all. The leader is determined. Martineau agrees with his course of action:

"When do you intend to convene the caucus and the Party?" he asks.

"Before February 20 when the new session opens. We'll meet at the Renaissance Club under the presidency of the great Thomas Chapais. The presence of this old family friend will surely restore my image in the eyes of those who would like to see me gone. I have made up my mind to lead the Opposition in the Legislative Assembly. Did anyone honestly think that I would leave politics? Only rats flee a sinking ship.

"The Union Nationale is in dire straits right now, but I am the only captain on board. I want to show the people that the Ottawa Liberals lied to them during their campaign with their silly promise of never bringing in conscription. I'm thinking of Ernest Lapointe when he was speaking at the Forum, which was absolutely packed. He threatened to leave the Party if ever Mackenzie King acted like Borden in 1917. The premier can't back down. The war is far from over.

"Do you know what is going on in Sorel? Pretty soon Marine Industries will receive an order to manufacture cannons. We're headed towards difficult times. Churchill is the one who said: 'Tears and blood will flow.'"

Martineau does not contradict his leader, but he has heard that Duplessis is not without reproach for his way of governing Quebec. A friend told him that Maurice led a dissolute life. Rumours are rife. Recently, he overheard this bit of gossip:

"We've lost count of the women the head of the Union Nationale is having one-night stands with. In the capital, it's an open secret: he meets prostitutes. And he drinks like a fish. The last parliamentary session was very difficult. That's probably why they want him to give up the leadership of the party."

Martineau thinks that one day soon he will speak to his leader, but for the moment, he shares the opinion of most MLAs: Duplessis is a fascinating, charismatic leader of whom much is forgiven. When meeting him, one is struck by his talent as a leader – and his ability to land on his feet.

"Taschereau rejoiced at my defeat," Maurice points out. "Good old Louis-Alexandre was the first one to congratulate Godbout. He thought he finally had his revenge, but the Liberals are a little too confident. As head of the Opposition, I intend to make life difficult for them."

"I can well believe that," quips Martineau, "but they say that recently you have had health problems. Are you feeling better now?"

"Oh, it's nothing. I treat my illness with a large gin. If it gets worse, I have a good doctor who can take care of me!"

∞

The sounds of war, at first distant, seem closer every day. They are nibbling at the borders. Already, 300,000 Canadians are in Europe fighting the enemy. The news, censored – which doesn't help – arrives late. It is invariably bad. People in Quebec have trouble understanding what is going on in Europe. In June 1940, people are horrified. France capitulates. Field Marshal Philippe Pétain signs an agreement with Hitler. Of course, there is this French general exiled in England who, on June 18, launches an appeal over the BBC to members of the Resistance. Nobody in Quebec really knows who Charles de Gaulle is.

In the morning when he wakes up, Maurice Duplessis always listens to the radio. In his suite at the

Château Frontenac, he gathers up the newspapers he leaves lying around so that he can read them at any time. He is passionate about current affairs. With his friends, he can discuss the international political situation for hours. Cynical, he sees dark days ahead for Canada. "De Gaulle is in league with Winston Churchill. You'll see these two bounce back. And when the United Kingdom needs men, she'll come here to get her cannon fodder."

Since his return to the Legislative Assembly in February, Duplessis has shown himself to be prudent and efficient. When Adélard Godbout took up his seat as head of the government, he proposed that women be given the vote. Duplessis was content to repeat Cardinal Villeneuve's objections. His speech was dull. He doesn't want to appear more aggressive than he has to be because he feels that women's emancipation is inevitable.

They are the ones working in the factories making bombs and ammunition for the war effort. Already, at Épiphanie, young girls are being recruited in great numbers. If women leave the home to work in factories, it is hard to see how they can be prevented from voting! And even if, on April 11, 1940, Duplessis speaks out against the bill that will give half the population the right to elect representatives in Quebec, he is aware that Thérèse Casgrain and Idola Saint-Jean are behind this victory. As a good politician, Maurice realizes that he will have to court the women's vote if he wants to be premier of the province again.

"Godbout is getting bogged down in his bills," he says to Gérald Martineau, whom he now addresses

with the less formal *tu* since he is part of the inner circle. "He is cutting farm credit, he wants to increase
taxes, and worse yet, he intends to attack public
schools. We'll soon have our chance, and Mackenzie
King will hand it to us on a silver platter. The spring
session was quiet enough, but summer is bound to
heat up.

"I never would have thought that the old Rouge
from Ottawa would pull off such a brilliant electoral
victory. Having the majority gives him a free hand to
impose the law on mobilizing national resources.

"A first step towards conscription – just like in
1917! Poor Adélard, he's so indebted to his big federal
cousin that he was obliged to vote against Chaloult's
motion to slow down King, who wants to involve
Canadians in the war at any price. It's not enough to
ration sugar and nylon stockings. He has to sacrifice
young people who can't find jobs. The economy has
been slow for ten years. It's easy to see that the poorest
have no choice but to sign up if they want to avoid
starving."

Martineau observes that the members reproach
the leader of the Union Nationale for his lack of enthusiasm during the debates at the Assembly. "Some are
even saying that Camillien Houde is stealing the lime-
light from you." Maurice agrees. The mayor of
Montreal likes to show off because he needs friends
among the Liberals. Godbout wants to put Montreal
under trusteeship because it can't repay its three-
million-dollar debt.

"Houde is a poor administrator who mixes politics
with theatre. Montreal is a city of easy pleasures. Its

red light district resembles Pigalle. In the old days, families used to live on Ontario Street. Nowadays, there are only strip clubs and bordellos. If you want a good address for smoking opium, or playing poker, or just to have a good time, there are dozens of places in the downtown area. Is that Camillien's pride and glory? And he would like us to take him seriously?"

Maurice doesn't fear Houde's presence in Quebec City. If he is acting less fiery than when he was sparring with Louis-Alexandre Taschereau, it is because he is still fretting over his defeat. One year in the Opposition has taught him to be silent and to speak only when necessary. He watches Premier Godbout, for whom he has a certain esteem. Both men are extremely courteous towards each other. But Duplessis is canny. He notes his adversary's mistakes so that he can lambaste him. During the summer of 1940, when Godbout approved Mackenzie King's move to amend the Constitution and to transfer monies from the unemployment fund to Ottawa, the leader of the Union Nationale heads the Quebec nationalist forces. *Finally a good point for me. May the next election come soon!* he thinks.

Saturday evening, when he finds himself in Montreal with friends, Maurice enjoys going to the Forum to take in a hockey game. Even if he has a marked preference for baseball, he often goes to the shrine on Atwater. He got his passion for hockey from Jean Barrette, a sports announcer, son of one of his MLAs, who gives him good tickets. A fan of the Canadiens team, Maurice grows animated and shouts along with the crowd when captain Hector "Toe" Blake gets a goal. He shoots, he scores! People are thrilled. This evening, he is in no mood to have fun, but the game against the Chicago Black Hawks helps him forget his dark thoughts for a few hours.

A few days ago, Paul Sauvé announced that he would be leaving for military service. Sauvé is a bit like the son Maurice never had. *He is my heir apparent*, Duplessis says to himself as if to distance himself from all those who are eyeing the position of leader of the Union Nationale. *But he's lazy. He could go farther if he wanted to.*

Paul trained in a military camp in hopes of going to war earlier. Nothing will prevent him from going to Europe. The Allied forces are being threatened. Maurice can understand this. He admires the young man, and when he gives him a hug, he reassures him:

"I saw Godbout yesterday. He confirmed to me that if ever he calls an early election, he would not field a candidate against you in the riding of Two Mountains. Go, Paul, my friend, and when you come back, your seat will be waiting for you."

After the hockey game, Maurice takes a taxi to the Ritz-Carlton, where he has an appointment with Gérald Martineau and Jos Bégin. The two men are cunning, at times even sly, and have made themselves indispensable within the Union Nationale. The three discuss politics until the bar closes. As MLA for Dorchester, a riding hard by the American border, Bégin is king of the castle. He is the very image of the powerful politician from the regions. A good organizer who is aware of everything that is going on, he lets his boss know how things stand regarding voters and events. A deputy after Duplessis's own heart.

In autumn 1940, while Field Marshal Pétain is preparing to meet Adolf Hitler in Montoire, here people are talking about Camillien Houde. Because he denounced the draft, the MLA from Sainte-Marie and mayor of Montreal was arrested on August 15 and taken to Petawawa Camp. Houde, wearing number 694, becomes a symbol of resistance. And this irritates Maurice, who looks upon the whole affair as a comedy to appeal to the gallery.

"Camillien knew perfectly well what he was doing when he spoke out against the federal decree, and now he would like us to cry over his fate," says Maurice.

As for Bégin, he remarks how the minister of justice, Ernest Lapointe, had to cut short his holidays and hurry back to Ottawa to sign the order of arrest.

"You seem to find that funny, Maurice," says Martineau.

"Every time the Liberal government makes a wrong move, we are closer to power," says Maurice. "Houde might look like a clown but he's someone we should keep on our side. Right now we've grown apart, but at the first opportunity, I intend to make peace with him. It's better to have him as a friend than as an enemy. His stay in Petawawa – I'm even going to call it his holidays – will make him into a martyr in the eyes of French Canadians. Camillien has become the figurehead of our resistance. I think it's time for me to get closer to him!"

Maurice orders another gin. He seems preoccupied. For one who likes to joke around with his friends, he's more serious than usual. "Godbout, the old devil! It seems it was quite a party, the inauguration of the Senneterre-Mont-Laurier highway! It's a lovely project that he managed to complete. I wish I had been the one behind it. If I had been in power longer, I would have opened up Abitibi, also. Many of our brave families have chosen to exile themselves up north rather than rot in the big city."

"Apparently, there are gold mines like in the Klondike," says Martineau.

"Come on. Let's be realistic! That's just public relations to get these poor wretches to go up north. The government needed strong arms to provide manpower for the big companies so they made us believe that Abitibi contains treasure. Do you honestly believe, Gerry, that the miners are getting rich digging around in the dirt? Did you ever read *Germinal* by Zola? You should because it's better than any history book. And I'm pretty sure that is what is going on in the gold mines of Rouyn."

Jos Bégin is surprised that his leader quotes a French writer.

"Do you realize what they say about you behind your back? That you have never opened a book in your life?"

"This reputation of lacking culture comes from those scribblers at *Le Devoir*. Listen to me, Jos, do you think I would be where I am if I hadn't received a proper education?" says Maurice.

"If I prefer to look like a simple man, it's because I want to feel close to the people. Only my close friends are aware that I have an appreciation for painting. Take

Cornelius Krieghoff, for example. Whenever I can, I buy one of his paintings. That is my real wealth. Our people don't want someone pretentious at the head of their government. Godbout is an agronomist, which is still acceptable, but his pinched look will eventually work against him. Not to mention Mackenzie King. An old bachelor who communicates with his mother through a crystal ball. He doesn't come across as being very serious, which is probably why people forgive him his bungling. As for me? I do everything I can to cover up my bourgeois upbringing. I read more than most of the people who accuse me of being ignorant. My favourite author is Mark Twain. He is incisive, a shrewd observer of American society. I studied Latin and Greek. I can decline *rosa, rosae, rosam*. I can quote Cicero in his diatribe against Catiline. But our people don't need me to make them feel small because of what I know. In any case, you already know what I think of intellectuals…"

Martineau and Bégin burst out laughing. Maurice starts poking fun at people again. He is particularly amused by Cardinal Villeneuve, who has distanced himself since the Rouges came to power. "His Eminence goes where the power is," he says, cynically. "He'll be back eating out of my hand again in a few years."

Martineau doesn't understand why Villeneuve approves of conscription. "He should hold his tongue like I do," says Duplessis. "The clergy shouldn't get mixed up in politics. He should be satisfied with serving the premier. It would be in Godbout's interest to keep the Cardinal in check like I did during my three years in power." Martineau agrees with his leader, but something has been bothering him now for some time:

"What do you think of the new archbishop of Montreal, Maurice?"

"Msgr. Joseph Charbonneau will never replace my old friend Georges Gauthier," says Duplessis. "I was very sad when he died last August. To tell you the truth, I don't trust Charbonneau. He is a Franco-Ontarian who was brought up in an orphanage. He likes the poor and he takes their side. I hope that he'll know his place. Well, it's getting pretty late. I'm going up to bed. Tomorrow, Abel will take us to Quebec City. We'll swing by my sister's house, where I promised to meet a few voters. I keep telling them that I have less influence now that I'm in the Opposition, but they still ask me to find them jobs."

Bégin advises him to get some rest.

"You look tired and you've aged."

"I don't know what's wrong with me, but sometimes I have a stomach ache. Maybe I should go and see the doctor. But I don't have time. Martineau, pay the bill, I'll reimburse you later."

7

I've Lost My Star

As a child, Maurice Duplessis liked nothing better than to go to Quebec City and see his father sit in the Legislative Assembly. Duplessis idolized his father. In his eyes, Nérée was equal to all the great explorers and pioneers whose adventures he was reading about in school. Ever since the days when he would run in the corridors looking for his father's office, the Assembly has felt like his private domain. When the train pulls into the station in Quebec City, it all comes rushing back to him – the memory of those happy days, the magic of those carefree feelings.

Maurice is overcome by nostalgia as he walks down Grande-Allée towards the walled city. The history of New France is carved into Quebec City's

Maurice Duplessis, the orator,
speaks to his electors.

landscape. Cape Diamond – that mammoth outcropping of rock, which Jacques Cartier saw rise up from the St. Lawrence River. And the Plains of Abraham, where the fate of the colony was sealed in thirteen short minutes.

As he crosses the threshold of the Legislative Assembly, Maurice can still hear his father's voice: "This is where Louis-Joseph Papineau led the fight to have the rights of French Canadians recognized. Louis-Joseph was Joseph's son. And one day they'll say of you: Maurice, son of Nérée."

This claim to a political dynasty was always been the ambition of the Duplessis family. And this ambition has never lessened over the years, a probable explanation for Maurice's bitterness as head of the Opposition. When people find him apathetic, he says: "I've lost my star." It is his way of saying that he is not the man he was in 1936.

Friends no longer hesitate to criticize him. At a meeting in Shawinigan, he created a scene when he was drunk. In Quebec City, during a reception at Chez Kerhulu Restaurant, he threw champagne glasses at the lamps. The staff had to hurry and clean up the mess. And all the car accidents. There have been so many that they are beyond counting.

At night, Maurice drives like a madman. Will scandal mar the end of his political career? How long will he have to live in the Liberal government's shadow? "I'm counting on Adélard Godbout's mistakes for our comeback," he keeps repeating.

His hopes are not entirely unreasonable. After all, the leader of the Rouges is trapped by world events. If Godbout were governing during a more peaceful era, he could probably deliver on his campaign promises. But in 1941, it doesn't look promising. Decidedly, the war is no longer strictly a European affair. Recently, the American Congress voted a budget of seven billion dollars to come to England's aid. Franklin Delano Roosevelt is even considering sending troops.

Today is Wednesday, and like every week, Maurice goes to the Basilica for the 6:30 a.m. Mass. And then he walks to the office. No sooner has he taken off his coat than he asks his secretary: "Do you have all the articles on the Rowell-Sirois Report?" Miss Auréa Cloutier brings them in and places them on top of the files. After a quick look at the newspapers, Duplessis phones Gérald Martineau:

"Did you see the first page of *Le Devoir*? Godbout is being accused of acting with servility. The federal-provincial conference called by Mackenzie King last January turned out to be a disaster for the premier. He didn't use the conference to push through the recommendations of the Rowell-Sirois Report on federal-provincial relations.

"I have been aware of King's little stratagem for a long time now. Ottawa wants to centralize power. It's in line with the war effort that is being asked of the provinces. It's all interconnected. Poor Adélard was fooled by it. He doesn't understand what is happening to him. He is digging his own grave. Provincial autonomy is the card that the Union Nationale will have to play. It's the ace that will help us win. The new tax structures that King is suggesting are a fraud, and I intend to expose him in the Assembly. I have to go. The session is beginning in a few minutes. I'll call you next

week. Between now and then, organize a meeting with
our Montreal MLAs to study the project of making the
St. Lawrence River navigable via a canal. It's important.
I have the impression that the province is being tricked,
but I'm not about to complain, Gerry, because it will
help tip the balance in our favour. See you tomorrow."

Miss Cloutier knocks at the door.

"Mr. Daniel Johnson to see you."

"Show him in."

A member of the Bar since 1940, Johnson is a kind
of golden boy and part of the Duplessis team. At the
next election, he will probably run in a riding where he
has a good chance of winning. The Chief has decided
he has talent, and immediately brought him into the
inner circle. A smart organizer who knows the area
around Acton Vale well, Johnson undertook to compile
the percentage of voters in several ridings. The numbers, which he analysed with Jos D. Bégin, show that
the Union Nationale has a solid base among the farmers
and regional notables. "The big push will be directed
towards the 20 per cent of undecided voters whom neither the Liberals nor our Party have succeeded in
attracting," he says. Duplessis warns him against an
excess of enthusiasm. The political situation shifts daily.
Right now there is not much hope on the horizon.

"Unfortunately, my dear Johnson, I must leave you
because the session starts in a few minutes and I have
many questions for the premier. The good thing about
the Opposition is that I can attack my adversary without causing too much trouble. But don't imagine that I
sit on my laurels, or that I work less. On the contrary,
I've had time to familiarize myself with the files

pertaining to education, the nationalization of electricity, external commerce, and taxation. When I was head of government, I was like a conductor who directed his players. Now, I'm learning the music and playing all the instruments. Being in the Opposition is an excellent school as long as you know how to await your turn. Mine is coming up and you'll be one of us, Daniel, and in a choice place, I give you my word!"

∞

When Mackenzie King learns that Quebec's most faithful representative in Ottawa, Ernest Lapointe, has cancer and that he only has a short time to live, he has a premonition that Lapointe's death will mark the end of an era during which Ottawa exercised a strong influence over Quebec. Who will replace Lapointe, the man mainly responsible for Duplessis's defeat in 1939? To replace him will not be easy.

"Guess who our dear prime minister is courting to replace Lapointe?" asks Martineau.

In his suite at the Ritz-Carlton Hotel, drink in hand, Gérald Martineau sits with Maurice Duplessis. The rumour has been circulating but today Martineau can confirm it:

"Mackenzie King is moving heaven and earth to get Adélard Godbout into the federal camp."

Maurice is one of the only ones who refuses to believe in this possibility.

"I'll bet you anything that Godbout will not go to Ottawa. Adélard doesn't have the stuff of a leader. He's a good man, he even has good ideas. I'm going to tell you something confidential: I would have liked to have him on my side, but I don't share his ideas on the future of Quebec," says Duplessis.

Maurice chews on the stub of his cigar and adds, laughing:

"In any case, Godbout could never be King's right-hand man... His English is too poor."

He continues:

"Gerry, do you want to hear an even better scoop? Louis Saint-Laurent is going to Ottawa to replace Ernest Lapointe. And let me tell you that this appointment is really good news for the Union Nationale!"

At the end of 1941, Duplessis's main preoccupation is his health. His doctor has ordered him to stop drinking and to get a more orderly lifestyle. Will he accept that he has to settle down? And to make matters worse, he has organized meetings all over the province. "I'm not about to cancel the speeches I'll be giving soon in Gaspésie. I'll rest after the Christmas holidays. Unless there are other appointments on my agenda."

But he is aware that his health problems are serious. He is feeling weak. At fifty-one, he feels very tired, a lassitude that obliges him to slow down his activities. Naturally, he doesn't complain. His friends advise him to take a holiday. "I went to Bermuda once, over ten years ago. I was bored out of my mind. I hate not doing anything," he replies curtly. He's not very athletic though sometimes he plays croquet, if only to please his English friends who are members of upper-crust clubs, especially in Hudson. He has put on weight, and his three-piece suits are getting rather tight. They make him look clumsy. Because he only measures

5 feet 8 inches, Duplessis is afraid of having a big stomach like Camillien Houde. People poke fun at Houde. He forces himself to take a daily walk. He walks between the Château Frontenac and the parliament buildings, greeting the many people who recognize him. He stops to speak to them, killing two birds with one stone. He never fails to sound out those who could eventually become voters. Duplessis lives for nothing but politics.

At the end of November an imposing funeral is held in honour of Ernest Lapointe. The mood of the country is dark. The funeral procession which leaves the Basilica of Quebec City to travel to Kamouraska in the lower St. Lawrence reflects the general mood of mourning felt by many of the citizens. It is wartime. Death is everywhere. On December 7, the Japanese attack Pearl Harbor. This marks the entrance of the United States into the war. Who can say when the massacre will end?

One night, when he is in Montreal, Maurice is subjected to a two-minute curfew. An alarm. Two minutes later, another siren. Is it a real attack? Have the Germans crossed the Atlantic? A third alarm. They are engulfed in a total blackout. The city is swallowed up in darkness. Suddenly, images of London during the Blitz come to mind. London under the rubble, with its houses burning. Is Montreal about to be destroyed? The last siren blasts a full two minutes. An eternity. At 10:47 p.m.! People are terrified. Will the next alarm announce a real attack?

At the Ritz-Carlton bar, Maurice chews on a Davidoff and gives a tip to the waiter who serves him another Singapore Sling. The orchestra plays the Glenn Miller hit "In The Mood." People are dancing the swing. What joy to be alive after experiencing a death scare!

∞

"Tell me what happened."

Adélard Godbout invites Jos Bégin, the Unioniste member from Dorchester, into his office.

"When I heard that Maurice Duplessis was hospitalized during the night, I thought you were one of the few who could give me news of your leader's health."

Looking tired and drawn, Jos Bégin is worried. The doctor has told him that Maurice is suffering from a strangulated hernia and that his convalescence will last several months.

"We were at the Château Frontenac when he suddenly felt ill. It was as if he couldn't breathe. He was choking and moaning. We called a doctor, and an ambulance. They operated that night. You know Maurice, he never complains. But at least he could have told us that he felt sick. Today, he's feeling a bit better."

"I'll go and see him. Please let me know when you have more news."

Like most of the elected members of the Union Nationale, Bégin is feeling lost. The session is opening in February. There is only one month to find someone who will replace the Chief during the debates in the Legislative Assembly. Almost automatically, the choice falls to Onésime Gagnon, whose personality is not flamboyant enough to stir up the waters.

It is understood that Maurice will continue to dictate his orders from his hospital bed. Dr. Florian Trempe is very strict: "You must rest until April. And not a drop of alcohol. Do you hear me, Mr. Duplessis? If not, you're finished and we won't be able to save you."

A shattering diagnosis. The year 1942 is off to a bad start. First there is the swearing off alcohol, like a sentence without appeal. And then political events are precipitated. There is a by-election on March 23 in Saint-Jean. Duplessis would have liked to campaign to gauge his party's strength against the Liberals. He had been gearing up for it since autumn, but he has to resign himself to remain in the shadow of Onésime Gagnon whom, fortunately, he trusts completely.

There isn't a day when Maurice doesn't receive visitors. His room at the Saint-Sacrement Hospital is like a second office. Today, the nurse announces the visit of Premier Adélard Godbout. The two men chat. Maurice takes the opportunity to congratulate his opponent for having refused Mackenzie King's offer to join the federal troops.

"You weren't made to sit in Ottawa. We might be political enemies, but I think you can be more effective in Quebec. You're like me, Adélard, you believe that it is only here in Quebec that we can see our ideas take shape. But I wouldn't like to be in your place. The federal government is going to force you to accept conscription. It's a pity, but you won't be able to avoid it."

Godbout hasn't come to see Duplessis to quarrel with him. And because he finds him lively and feisty whenever there is an idea to debate, the Liberal premier thinks Maurice Duplessis will be around for a long time yet.

"You're indestructible, my dear Duplessis. Politics is bringing you around," he says, mockingly, before leaving the room.

∞

After a four-month convalescence, Maurice Duplessis returns to the Assembly in April. Despite the Union Nationale's defeat in the Saint-Jean by-election, he begins the second half of his mandate with enthusiasm, sure of an eventual victory over the Liberals. Everything unfolds as planned. Pressured by powerful financial lobby groups who want Canada to increase its war effort, Mackenzie King announces that there will be a national plebiscite. In his office at the Legislature, Maurice is with Gérald Martineau who, as party treasurer, often meets with the Chief. He has prepared envelopes with fifty dollars in each envelope to reward journalists who write positively about the Union Nationale.

"I also gave a little gift of one hundred dollars to your nurse. Her discretion is worth it, don't you agree?"

Maurice approves of his lieutenant's actions. In politics, one has to know where to place one's money in order to see it bear fruit.

"Did you see the question Mackenzie King concocted for the plebiscite?"

Martineau brandishes a document and reads out loud:

Do you agree to release the government from any obligation resulting from prior engagements on restricting how the troops are mobilized for military service?

"Can you imagine a more complicated or hypocritical question? Canadians have been encouraged for a long time now to vote 'Yes.' I have the impression that Quebec will have to work really hard to reverse this trend."

Martineau, who is just back from spending a few days in Montreal, tells his leader that a group of people, mostly young people, have formed a movement, la Ligue pour la défense du Canada [the League for the Defence of Canada].

"Yes, I know about it," says Duplessis. "Our friend Paul Gouin is behind it, and he is recruiting members from the Ordre de Jacques Cartier. Have you ever heard of La Patente? It's a secret society founded in 1926 by French-Canadian civil servants who modelled themselves on the Washington Irish and their Knights of Columbus. The Ordre de Jacques Cartier is our Knights of Columbus – francophone, nationalist, and Catholic."

What Maurice fears most is that this group will eventually form a political party.

"I have always said three parties in Quebec is one too many. Especially since these new adversaries will try to win over our nationalist supporters. We have to keep an eye on them. Do you have their names?"

"My list is incomplete. Apart from Gouin, the most active militants are Maxime Raymond, René Chaloult, Philippe Hamel. There is also André

Laurendeau and some new ones, good speakers, like Jean Drapeau, a Montreal lawyer, and Michel Chartrand, a union leader who fires up the crowds. Some say that their movement is not serious..."

"Careful, Martineau. The political world is undergoing total transformation. It's not like in 1936 when I was able to oust poor old Gouin, who was busy writing his poetry! Today, people are feeling threatened. War is at our doorstep. We can't delude ourselves. If the League for the Defence of Canada is successful, we will have to organize very quickly. Those people are playing in our bailiwick. Their supporters also happen to be ours. And I have no intention of being robbed of the rewards of my work. I would like you to hire people who will report back to us everything that is being said at their meetings."

Maurice wants to check out for himself the rumours that are circulating about this movement, which seems very popular in Montreal and Quebec City, but once again, health problems force him to slow down. Shortly after his return to the Assembly, he finds himself back in hospital. His diabetes is getting worse. His physician tells him: "Mr. Duplessis, you will have to give yourself daily shots of insulin for the rest of your life."

This is very bad news! Being ill is the worst kind of publicity for a politician. How will he hide this liability? The year 1942 is a desperate one for Maurice's entourage because the illnesses keep on piling up. He is an inveterate smoker, and is not able to recover from a bout of pneumonia complicated by consumption. Maurice has to go under the oxygen tent several times.

He turns this difficulty to his advantage. The experience provides him with an image he can use.

"I am like Quebec," he likes to repeat at every opportunity, "We both need pure air."

He might like to joke but these long periods away from active politics make him vulnerable to betrayal. Within the Union Nationale, people are grumbling. There are men out there who would like to foment a plot to replace this leader who is absent much too often. When Maurice learns that Paul Sauvé has set himself up at the military base in Farnham and is trying to rally supporters, he explodes. His anger is equal to the friendship he feels for his protégé. He jumps up and runs to the phone:

"How dare you say that I'm only a drunk? I'll have you know, my dear Paul, that I am finished with alcohol. I have news for those who thought I was dead and buried : I'm coming back and I'm here to stay. Let it be said once and for all!"

As soon as he feels well enough, Duplessis makes the round of several provincial towns. He delivers his best speeches during these meetings, where people feel like a big family and everyone is a friend. Riding high on the hurrahs, he criticizes the Liberals, ridicules them, demonizes them. The equation is simple: Godbout is the puppet of Mackenzie King, for whom Quebec doesn't count in the federal game. Maurice says what his fellow citizens want to hear. He is a nationalist and is anti-conscription. In the Gaspé, at Lac-Saint-Jean, everywhere he goes he ignites passions and gives the impression that he has the power to reverse the situation. Among those who come out to see the leader of the Opposition are many who regret not having voted for the Bleus and are convinced that Duplessis could save the province, that he is the only one strong enough to stand up to Mackenzie King, who can't be trusted!

When he returns to Quebec City, Maurice spends a few days at the Château Frontenac. From his suite, which resembles the headquarters of a major state, he directs the actions of his supporters. Now that he has given up alcohol, he drinks litres of orange juice compulsively. He pokes fun at himself: "It's not as good as gin, but it's better for my health."

Duplessis often works until after midnight. On August 18, 1942, Maurice is awakened by the phone. It's Gérald Martineau. "Turn on the radio, Maurice. Read the newspaper. Thousands of Canadians have been killed in Dieppe!"

The Canadian population is in a state of shock. The raid on the cliffs of Normandy is an unimaginable disaster. The attack, which had been kept secret up until the last minute, turned out to be a dismal failure. The country is in mourning and this time people can't escape the truth that Canada is directly affected by the war. German machine-guns have killed our youth, and everyone's prayers are being offered for those who left their lives on the beaches of France.

In the following hours, news of the massacre is confirmed. The first photos show bodies riddled with bullet holes, cadavers sleeping under piles of shells. At Quebec City's Basilica, Maurice Duplessis attends

Mass with Premier Godbout, a Mass that pays tribute to the thousands of soldiers who will never return home. Summer is almost over. It is a gloomy and grey time. No one thinks that the war, this funny kind of war as they first called it, will ever end.

On October 11, 1942, en route to Quebec City, Maurice finds out that a new political party will present itself at the next election. Just as he thought, the Ligue pour la defense du Canada has folded, only to emerge as the Bloc Populaire Canadien.[1] Duplessis phones Martineau: "These ranters are in league with the Liberals. It's a plot from Ottawa." He is furious. They have to find a way to shoot down this rare bird headed for success. Should he be worried? The next provincial election is in two years. He feels there is enough time for him to dig in and fight his opponents. He is not impressed with the *bloquistes*. "We have to redouble our efforts," he says to his troops. "They are birdbrains who have cooked up a political party, but we have tradition on our side."

When the session reopens, Adélard Godbout is heading a government that is foundering badly. The decisions Mackenzie King has imposed have undermined the Quebec Liberals. Since the April plebiscite of 1942, the gap has widened between the only francophone province and the rest of Canada. There are two solitudes in the country, and each has voted according to their conscience. The results are there to prove it: 63 per cent of Canadians are willing to release the federal government from its anti-conscription

1. An anti-conscription wartime Quebec party.

promises. But 72 per cent of Quebecers vote "No," indicating their refusal to support legislation aimed at sending conscripts overseas. The division is sharp: two opposing visions.

At a time when the world conflict is spilling over its European borders, Canada's ethno-linguistic spats are masking international reality. But the fate of the West is being played out in the port of Stalingrad on the banks of the Volga. The Soviets are engaged in a ferocious battle with the Germans. If the war continues, Quebecers will have to put aside their resistance and resign themselves to wear the uniform and bear arms.

"In 1917, the RCMP even went into the countryside to ferret out the most rebellious deserters who were hiding there. Some of them went so far as to disguise themselves as women to avoid being dragged away." Maurice tells his friends that the wealthy are paying the poor to take their place in the regiments. "Those who have never experienced war can't understand the meaning of despair. I didn't think I would ever live to see such a mess again!"

In the car bringing him back to the capital, Maurice looks out at a group of young volunteers marching by. That afternoon, as usual, hundreds of Montrealers, with their Union Jacks fluttering in the wind, are gathered on the sidewalks to wave to a contingent of soldiers advancing along Sherbrooke Street. In the distance, they can be seen in tight khaki ranks, marching in step. That evening, they will ship out on their way across the Atlantic. And tonight, soldier Lebrun will sing *Je suis loin de toi, Mignonne* [I am far from you, my darling].

When the session re-opens at the Legislative Assembly, the atmosphere is heavy and rife with sadness. Godbout, who feels the mounting anger against his government, is determined to push through the laws he considers important before the next electoral campaign. Agriculture, industry, and especially education are areas that he has targeted. He wants to implement change. In the early 1940s, over fifty thousand children are not registered in the schools. The situation in Quebec is deplorable, especially when compared to the anglophone provinces.

In 1943, Liberal MLA Hector Perrier tables a bill for compulsory education for children between the ages of six and fourteen. "I'm against it!" Duplessis angrily opposes the measure. "Parents alone are responsible for their children's education. If they want to keep them at home or send them out to work, that is their right." The head of the Union Nationale is angry. He accuses the Liberals of being the enemies of Catholicism because they want to impose a secular system of education. But in vain. The Union Nationale is a minority and is unable to stop the law from passing. This infuriates Duplessis. "I have the impression that Godbout wants to make his mark. I didn't think he was this subtle a politician. I'm surprised."

Does he fear him? "No," he confides to his friends, "I know he is up against a much tougher adversary than me – the war! When it comes time to vote, nobody will forgive him for his attitude during this worldwide conflict."

The note, signed by a commanding officer of the RCMP, is an order: Mr. Maurice Duplessis must give up his suite at the Château Frontenac. It is mid-August and Quebec City is in a state of excitement. Winston Churchill and Franklin Delano Roosevelt are coming to Quebec City. The two greatest leaders of the free world are meeting to discuss a last offensive against Adolf Hitler. The Quebec Conference is an opportunity for Mackenzie King to present himself as a statesman. Canada, hosting the prime minister of Great Britain and the president of the United States, is positioning itself among the powerful. Duplessis doesn't think much of this masquerade. However, being courteous, he agrees to move out.

"You want me to give up my room to Admiral Dudley Pound, Churchill's friend! I demand that this receipt be signed. I have three boxes of records, eight boxes of books, a Larousse dictionary, and an Encyclopedia Britannica. I want to find these objects where I left them, do you understand?"

These little manias of a confirmed bachelor cause the commander-in-chief of the RCMP to smile. "Have no fear, Mr. Duplessis; Admiral Pound is a most trustworthy guest. But if ever after his departure you were missing a book or a record, we hold ourselves responsible for any theft."

The conference in Quebec City is a good opportunity for Mackenzie King to be visible in the world press. During the social events, he seizes the opportunity to brag that Canada is hosting the event, not Quebec. Adélard Godbout, more discreet, remains in the shadow of his federal cousin. As leader of the

Opposition, Duplessis mingles with the socialites who are anxious to be photographed with Roosevelt or Churchill. The grand ballroom of the Château Frontenac has never seen so many diamonds, plunging necklines, and tuxedos. It is like a spectacular Hollywood film featuring Fred Astaire and Ginger Rogers, the greatest stars of the era.

At the head table, Churchill draws on his cigar and savours his scotch. Not far from him, someone else is also smoking with pleasure – Maurice, with a Larenada in the corner of his mouth. He is preoccupied. He is not in the mood to be bored in Quebec City. He intends to leave fairly soon to tour the province. Two gulps of orange juice, a pat on the back from a cabinet minister who recognizes him, and he goes off to bed. This evening he will call his friends to pick him up at dawn.

∽

"In 1937, when I was in power, I received a letter from a certain Von Ribbentrop who wanted to buy Anticosti Island. Can you imagine – he wanted to install German scientists on our doorstep."

Maurice Duplessis is speaking on the stage of a church basement in the Eastern Townships. He addresses his crowd of supporters passionately. For the nth time, he recounts this anecdote to underscore the wisdom of his decision taken six years earlier when he was premier of Quebec.

"If I had accepted, do you know where we would be today? Do you know who Von Ribbentrop is? Yes,

yes, he is Hitler's right-hand man, a member of the SS who tortures our men overseas! If I had been a coward, today Quebec would be contaminated with Nazi vermin. It is not Godbout who can brag about such foresight. No, ladies and gentlemen, the leader of the Liberal Party allowed Mackenzie King to mislead you with his plebiscite."

Well before the official announcement of the election, Duplessis is already on the campaign trail. Often accompanied by Abel Vineberg, he asks Gérald Martineau, treasurer of the Union Nationale, to drive him to the farthest corners of the province. Maurice is tireless. In the morning, he shakes hands with the voters at a breakfast in his honour. At noon, he meets with labourers at their worksite. In the evening, he triumphs with fiery speeches. Impulsive and flamboyant, he festoons his oratory with witticisms that often narrowly miss being insolent.

He invents a new word game with Bona Arsenault's name, the former ally turned foe: "*Il faut que Bona ... parte!*" [Bona must go.] And everyone chuckles. Another time he recounts how he told his counterpart from Ontario what the expression "*chef de cabinet*" means. Adopting a serious tone of voice, Maurice explains: "It's the guy who pulls the chain when I go to the bathroom." And the whole hall breaks up.

Maurice is trying to curry favour just like in the old days when he used to poke fun at Taschereau. Little by little, he weighs his chances of success. They appear good. Martineau assures him: people are coming to hear him by the hundreds because they are disappointed with the Godbout government. And they intend to show the Liberals the door when it comes time to vote. Nothing seems to stop the wave of confidence that Duplessis is inspiring.

When Godbout calls the election for August 8, 1944, the Liberal premier has no illusions. The Union Nationale is one length ahead. Time is kind to Duplessis's men. The measures voted in by the Liberals have caused so much dissatisfaction among the people that it would take a miracle to reverse the trend. Duplessis, welcomed as a hero and hailed as the defender of French Canadians, squashes Godbout, who is booed by the people. They hold him responsible for all the evils in the province. At a time when everything is in short supply – when meat, butter, and sugar are rationed – the electorate accuses the government of doing nothing to improve the situation. Duplessis now has the upper hand. He allows history to take its course. Sometimes, he openly criticizes laws passed in haste by the Liberal government:

"In October 1943, Godbout nationalized Montreal Light, Heat and Power. Let me tell you: those Rouges are Communists!"

Duplessis sees enemies everywhere. In Europe, there are the Nazis, the Brown Shirts, the Fascists, the Communists, Stalin, Hitler, and Mussolini. In Quebec, they are everywhere and nowhere. Paranoia prevails. And what have Godbout and the intellectuals done? Duplessis brands them with the same iron. They are the bad guys, the ones that are out to destroy the harmonious society that used to exist, the one that people feel nostalgic for. He promises that with the Union

Nationale in power, the people won't have to fear social upheaval.

"Nationalization of electricity is a Bolshevik project," he says to the crowds, reiterating once again his famous slogan: "Electors – electricity!" Supporters applaud. The people ask for more. Maurice Duplessis is in step with the times. He is against the big federal cousin, against industrialization, which will destroy the rural cocoon, against a world mired in a never-ending conflict. The Union Nationale Party manages to convince Quebecers that Duplessis can protect them from all the evils of the planet. Maurice Duplessis is reassuring.

On August 8, 1944, the early results of the provincial election confirm the victory of the Union Nationale. The Liberals come in strong in Quebec City and Montreal, but elsewhere, in the regions, the number of Bleu ridings is increasing. As the evening progresses, Adélard Godbout's defeat is no longer in doubt. More than four hours after the polls close on Saint-Jacques Street, the large billboard on the building of the newspaper *La Presse* reads: Victory of the Union Nationale. Maurice Duplessis, new Premier of Quebec.

Maurice Duplessis (around 1950) with Gratien Gélinas
(third from left). Gélinas is now considered one of the founders
of modern Canadian theatre and film.

Maurice Duplessis inaugurates a bowling alley (around 1954).

8

Power and Nothing But Power

"I never doubted we would win, but it did get a little tricky!"

Maurice, with Gérald Martineau, is reviewing the results of the election. After four years in the Opposition, the Union Nationale is back in power, although they have only 38 per cent of the popular vote as against 40 per cent for the Liberals. The electoral map, with its many ridings outside the urban centers, favoured Duplessis. And what of the women who voted for the first time in Quebec's history?

"The majority of them voted for us," reassures Martineau. "Apparently, they didn't appreciate Godbout's government despite his gift to them."

"Women, Gerry, are the guardians of the home. They are the ones who look after the well-being of the family. They are the ones who see that there is food on the table. When a government rations essential foods and a mother has to count the quarts of milk she buys, you can't hope to win! On the one hand, Godbout forced children to remain on the school benches. On the other, he obliged everyone to tighten their belts.

"And the Bloc Populaire ended up being a straw fire: four members, that's far from being a landslide victory.

"I always took the members of the party seriously, though. André Laurendeau, their leader, doesn't have the stuff to be a premier, but he's a good fighter, a talented journalist. He might look like a seminarian but he's a great orator who succeeded in attracting many supporters. Do you remember the rally at the Royals Stadium on De Lorimier Avenue?"

"The one where Henri Bourassa gave his support to the Bloc?" asks Martineau.

"Yes, yes. Well, despite the tramway strike, twenty thousand people came to hear Laurendeau. They say that the Bloc was caught off guard when Godbout called the election. The Bloc's real problem lies elsewhere. In politics, it's always the same story: lack of money. Their electoral coffers never contained more than forty thousand dollars. You don't go very far with that! And the Bloc Populaire is insisting on running candidates in Ottawa," says Duplessis.

"The Union Nationale's strength comes from the fact that we concentrate our efforts in Quebec," he continues. "We're not scattered like the Liberals or the

Bloquistes. We are unique: *La belle province* is our territory. The party that I founded almost ten years ago has taken root everywhere in the province, and the tree's roots have spread. It can no longer be cut down. It is like an oak tree. It resists the storms."

Buoyed by his victory, Maurice is convinced that he is always right.

It is always a wonderful moment when he takes the time to savour a cigar just as he would savour good wine. After examining the tip, he contemplates the thickness of the outer leaves. A delicious ritual, as delightful as the flavours he can taste in advance.

"You see, Gerald, I was able to stop drinking, even if the temptation is always there, but no doctor will ever stop me from smoking. Did you know that every cigar has its own personality?"

Closing his eyes, he sniffs the Davidoff.

"Mmmmm! What an aroma. It smells like the Southern Isles, it's a superb cigar! I'm not like Camillien who smokes Palinas at two for fifteen cents! By the way, any news of our old enemy?"

With a slice of the guillotine, he snips the tip of the cigar without bruising the body. Martineau gets up, lighter in hand.

"Wait a minute! The gas will ruin the taste and the perfume. Do you have any matches? The trick is to light the inside of the cigar where it's been cut so that the flame does not come into contact with the skin. And, once it starts to glow like an ember, you start inhaling short little puffs of happiness."

Maurice sinks into his armchair. He loses himself in thought. He has regained power, and he intends to hold on to it. This second chance is a gift. From now on, he will make his mark; impose his style and his personality.

∞

On August 16, 1944, a train rolls into Windsor Station, after making a stop in Saint-Hyacinthe. Hundreds of people are waiting on the platform to see the person about to emerge from the coach. A journalist cries out: "There he is!" Photographers rush over. After four years in an internment camp, Camillien Houde is given a hero's welcome. Montreal is celebrating his return. He waves to the crowds from the car bringing him to his home on Saint-Hubert Street. He is the man who personifies the resistance to conscription.

In Quebec City, in his office in the parliament buildings, Duplessis has gathered together a few friends. He must find a way to make peace with Houde, whose prestige is most annoying to him. "Arrange a meeting with him. I'm ready to pretend that I like him so that he will not make it difficult for us. I'm even ready to help get him get re-elected as mayor in December. Please arrange a reconciliation as soon as possible!"

In the House, Duplessis falls back into his old habits. The orator rises, his MLAs listen to him and applaud his performances. The Liberals are now relegated to the thankless role of the Opposition. The progressive measures they had put forward during their last mandate have now been cast aside. This does not, however, undermine the good relations between

Maurice Duplessis and Adélard Godbout. At the end of autumn, the latter offers Duplessis a basketful of apples from his orchard in Frelighsburg: "This way, Maurice, at least you'll appreciate my talent as an agronomist even if you think that I made a poor premier!"

At the opening of the session, the provincial government moves cautiously, caught up in the horror of the world situation. In fact, Quebecers are more interested in the latest news from Europe. They are afraid that one day Mackenzie King will introduce conscription, which has already been approved by the vote of April 1942. *The Commando's Fiancée* is the most popular radio series. The Huns are wicked and, luckily, they are about to be crushed. Just like in real life. Since the Normandy landing, Nazi lunacy is in its death throes.

Like all Quebecers, Maurice remembers the moment when the news broke. It was one of the greatest events of the times. On June 6, 1944, less than a year ago, the Atlantic Wall, built by the Germans as a fortification during their occupation of France, had been scaled. Yes, victory was just around the corner. On the ground, war correspondents were sending messages that always arrived a bit late, communications being so precarious. But, at the end of the day, on the air waves of Radio-Canada, Roger Baulu's voice confirmed that the Allies, under American General Dwight D. Eisenhower, had taken the French coastline by force, that the troops of the Free Forces were marching into occupied territory, and that soldiers were advancing, ready to do battle for France – the battle that would seal the fate of the Western conflict.

Among these brave men were some of our own French Canadians, in their khaki uniforms, with rifles on their shoulders and fear gripping their stomachs.

In his hotel room, Duplessis has followed closely the stages of the Landing. Today, with Martineau, he is discussing the possible outcome. They ask themselves the same question: soldiers are dying by the thousands, nameless, under German fire at Omaha Beach. Will the others, the survivors of this massacre, succeed in liberating Paris after pushing their way through the French countryside? Maurice is convinced of one thing: Mackenzie King is caught in a trap. "The Normandy Landing is the beginning of the end," he explains to Martineau, who shows himself to be more cautious. "Despite the Allied victory, I predict that before long Ottawa will have to make a final war effort. In order to carry out the fatal attack, Canada will have to send more troops overseas. But this time they will be draftees. And we, the Unionistes, will not be dirtied by this painful political decision."

Duplessis was right. A departmental order issued on November 23, 1944 by Mackenzie King's Liberal government obliges sixteen thousand young people to sign up to fight in Europe. The year ends as it began, with tears and curses. And people are asking themselves, despairingly, when will this craziness, which started five years ago, finally end?

Few remember Danzig, which the Third Reich invaded in September 1939. So much time has passed and so many crises have occurred that people have almost forgotten this port city situated at the mouth of the Vistula. The attack on Danzig was the initial pretext that triggered the Second World War. Europe, which used to seem so far away, is holding Quebec in a vise-like grip.

∞

Every morning, Maurice Duplessis goes to the barber-shop at the Château Frontenac. Sunk into his chair, he allows himself to be shaved while speaking with the habitués, the MLAs who are his friends, members of his own party but also Liberal members. The ambiance is light-hearted, there is laughter, people poke fun at one another, exchange the hottest gossip. Then, on a more serious note, they discuss recent events. Since Yalta, when Churchill, Roosevelt, and Stalin divided up the planet according to their respective appetites, a new world order is taking shape. But the crowning event is the day when the enemy surrenders.

On May 8, 1945, "God Save the King" keeps breaking in during special programs. "And they also play '*Ça sent si bon la France*' [And France smells so sweet] sung by Maurice Chevalier," adds Duplessis. Chevalier is one of his favourite singers. Churchill's photograph is in all the newspapers. As usual, he is making a V for victory with his index and middle finger. Only this time it has come to pass. The nightmare is finally over. And now for the promise of peace. At the price of many tears and doubts, the Allies have finally won against the forces of evil.

Goebbels, who committed suicide after killing his six children, the concentration camps discovered in

Dachau and elsewhere – all this will forever remain as scars, open wounds in the sunshine of victory. The Second World War can be summed up as a bloody episode in a grotesque tragedy played out in the human theatre. In Quebec, the only subject of conversation is the return of the soldiers. In a few weeks, ships will be bringing the troops back home.

With the war over, Maurice feels that he can finally occupy the place on the Canadian political scene that is rightly his.

"Mr. Duplessis, do you think that Mackenzie King will be re-elected prime minister of Canada?"

The barber shapes the contour of the moustache of his most illustrious client, a slim little brush above the upper lip.

"My dear friend, King has been reigning in Ottawa for the past twenty years. But he is very sick, and Louis Saint-Laurent will replace him as head of the Liberal Party. For me, it is six of one and half a dozen of the other. It's all the same."

Seated not far from Duplessis is a member of the Opposition who finds him somewhat of a braggart. "Did you know that in France women have only now been given the vote? And to think that you opposed our leader Adélard Godbout, a visionary, who gave Quebec women the right to vote five years ago!"

"Wait a minute," says Duplessis. "My projects for women and families are even more daring. The crumbs that King sends us from his big budget feel like charity. A-U-T-O-N-O-M-O-U-S, do you know what that means? This is my slogan: I intend to repatriate the money that is rightfully ours."

"Do you want Quebec to separate?" the member asks.

"No, I just want what the British North America Act granted us when the Fathers of Confederation signed it back in 1867," replies Duplessis. "Have you ever read articles 91 and 92?"

Duplessis can go on forever when it comes to the Constitution. Once again he becomes the lawyer who used to plead his cases. He reels off from memory such and such a document that he compares to a study whose arguments he has not forgotten.

The barber bends over him with his shaving brush:

"Mr. Duplessis, please, a few moments of silence. I need to soap your face."

∞

When the week's work is over in the Legislative Assembly, Maurice takes time to put his files in order. He phones Miss Cloutier to make sure that she will have everything ready for him on Monday morning. "I'll be here before eight. In the meantime, take the calls and don't forget to underline the names of people who donate generously to the Union Nationale. Send congratulations to Mr. Labrie, who has just won first prize at the Agricultural Fair in Saint-Hyacinthe. He's a real Bleu; find a few words to praise his livestock!"

Then Maurice, tired, climbs into the car with Vineberg and Martineau and heads off to Montreal. He stops at Trois-Rivières, at his sister's, to spend a few hours receiving voters in his office located in the basement of her house. Despite being premier, he has no intention of changing his thirty-year-old habits. The weekly meetings with people from his riding allow him to gauge their degree of satisfaction.

This afternoon, he is meeting with Mr. Lalande, a small businessman from Trois-Rivières who is interested in a construction project in the riding. For Duplessis, rewarding those who are faithful to the Union Nationale is all part of politics. His fiercest opponents use the word *blackmail*. Maurice is not bothered by this. "My dear Lalande," he says to his Unioniste friend, "I trust you, I know that you will do good work. Next week, call upon my minister of public works, who will sign your contract. You deserve it."

In a few minutes, the deal is sealed, confirmed with a handshake. Maurice accompanies his guest to the door, all the while reminding him not to forget to contribute to the Party. The ritual is out in the open. When Duplessis helps someone, he expects the favour to be returned.

The premier keeps the electoral fund of his riding in his office. At the back of a small cupboard he has hoarded sixty thousand dollars in small denominations. A reasonable sum of money, he feels. This way if a voter needs help, he can give him a hand. For instance, today the owner of a small business on Laviolette Street came to see him because he badly needed one hundred and fifty dollars. After he left, Maurice called in his secretary and discussed the matter. Should he or should he not lend him that much money? Auréa Cloutier gives good advice, Maurice trusts her judgment. He finally gives the go-ahead.

"Miss Cloutier, Monday afternoon, give an envelope to Mr. Louis Leclerc. And add his name to the list of people to whom the Union Nationale gave a loan this year."

∞

When Paul Ribbets, who was piloting the *Elona Gay*, dropped the atomic bomb "Little Boy" on Hiroshima on August 6, 1945 at 8:13 a.m., the world was struck with horror. An image emerges, that of a cloud in the shape of a mushroom. From now on, nuclear destruction threatens the planet. It is the ultimate terror. Those who have the atomic bomb are masters of the universe. But little by little, a secret is unveiled: the Americans do not have a monopoly on the devil's arsenal. In the Soviet Union, Stalin can perhaps blow up any city on the planet if he so chooses. He could do it on a whim. In a memorable speech given at the University of Missouri, Winston Churchill coins a pithy phrase designating the new political order. Between the free world and the Communist countries, there is now an Iron Curtain.

Where is the enemy? He hides behind a benevolent mask. What colour is he? Red (Rouge), like hellfire.

In Quebec, this way of thinking becomes quickly ingrained. For a long time now, Maurice Duplessis has considered Communists to be undesirable, a veritable cancer in society. For him, the equation is simple: they are making inroads in the unions, and their influence is dangerous. There are a growing number of people among these agitators who are dissatisfied with the capitalist regime. With their revolutionary ideas, these Communists – or *communisses* – as Duplessis likes to call them, are undermining the power of management, the very foundation of Quebec society. Why are union leaders demanding improved working conditions and salary raises?

Maurice is angry when he attacks these lunatics who could undermine the confidence of the investors. The bosses are his friends. Mr. Jules Timmins, vice-president of Iron Ore, is one of the people he often invites to dinner at the Château Frontenac. In the pre-mier's opinion, it is not the right moment to scare off the wealthy. It is better to take advantage of the growth in the economy brought on by the end of the war. And to silence those bent on making demands.

The Chief wants to reign in an atmosphere of order and submission. No discordant voices to disturb the harmony.

In order to do this, Maurice Duplessis sets about consolidating his power. As premier of Quebec, he takes on the job of attorney general – and he is a very forceful one – and also directs intergovernmental affairs. As head of the Union Nationale, he is also min-ister of justice. This multiplicity of tasks allows him to have a free hand in his ministers' departmental affairs and to squash any adversary who might wish to harm him. He revives the Padlock Law, still on the books since his first mandate, and orders the provincial police to put a lock on the door of the headquarters of the Communist paper *Le Combat*, located at 263 Sainte-Catherine Street East.

He is pursuing a fixed idea, and has a new bill in mind. He wants to carry out a major cleanup that will eliminate his opponents. It is late 1946, and Maurice is worried. The Jehovah's Witnesses irritate him to the highest degree. He sees this religious movement as a public nuisance, and their arrogance as a threat to the Catholic Church. In his office in the Assembly, Duplessis meets with Hilaire Beauregard, chief of the provincial police. They work for weeks on a plan that would put an end to public solicitation by the Jehovah's Witnesses. He is furious to discover that a good many of these fanatics whom he sent to jail are now out free.

"It seems that a certain Frank Roncarelli has put up bail for 396 Witnesses convicted by our tribunals! What's this all about?" asks Duplessis.

"Roncarelli is the owner of a restaurant on Crescent Street, the Quaff Café," replies Beauregard.

"Does he sell liquor?" asks Duplessis.

"Yes…"

"As attorney general for the province, I have the power to initiate proceedings against anyone who endangers Quebec society. I don't want to see any more Jehovah's Witnesses on street corners, with their flyers and their innocent faces, harassing our poor people. I want peace and I will get it. There is a law in Quebec that allows me to remove the liquor permit from those who do not respect order and justice. I have asked Judge Archambault, of the Liquor Commission, to sign a warrant so that I can take action against this suspicious character. The police will go and clean up the place. I want to put an end to this situation," says Duplessis.

Maurice thinks he has won. He doesn't know that this affair will drag on for ten more years. Frank Roncarelli is not a man who capitulates easily. He's not afraid of legal battles, and after initiating proceedings, the businessman eventually comes out the winner against the premier. In March 1956, a sheepish Duplessis has to pay out forty-seven thousand dollars in damages, which the Union Nationale generously advances. But Roncarelli is ruined and goes into exile in the States.

Maurice Duplessis gets caught in a trap of his own making. His crusade against the Jehovah's Witnesses is a failure. It exposes a character trait that will eventually land him in a lot of trouble: his unreasonable stubbornness in wanting to destroy a tough opponent. In fact, this proud man, who is also a poor loser, never admits his wrongs. Engaged in conflicts that he often creates, Duplessis thinks he can govern like certain premiers before him, dictating laws and imposing silence. A prisoner of his convictions, he refuses to compromise. He never backs down. A man of power, he constantly fears losing this power and obsesses almost to the point of paranoia. Those who do not share his opinions are automatically his enemies. Over the years, his fear of a plot outweighs his common sense.

Despite the yoke of an authoritarian premier, Quebec is definitely on the road to emancipation. Ideas continue to circulate despite the police padlocking of places where the demon of subversion is said to lurk. Maurice Duplessis is still at the height of his legend but an intellectual elite is starting to emerge despite all the restrictions.

In Quebec City, a Dominican priest, George-Henri Lévesque, founds a new faculty where social sciences will be taught. Politics, sociology, and economics are also on the curriculum. The students enrolled in these courses are discovering new horizons. In Montreal, the magazine *La Relève*, which has existed since the end of the ten-year economic crisis that started in 1929, is bucking the dominant ideology. The magazine has attracted a group of young people who are trying to break free of tradition. Hector de Saint-Denys Garneau speaks of painting and poetry while Robert Charbonneau tries to define Quebecers in relation to the rest of humanity.

At the end of the Forties, Quebec, still incubating these ideas, wants nothing more than to join the modern world. In less than ten years, another generation will be at the forefront of the scene. Maurice Duplessis, who wants to keep Quebec in its backward-looking cocoon, finds himself facing protests that he can't quash.

After meeting with his cabinet, the leader of the Union Nationale takes Martineau aside. He has something important to tell him. Next Sunday, he is meeting with Camillien Houde.

"The historian Robert Rumilly arranged our reconciliation."

"Are you still convinced that what you are doing is for the best?" asks Martineau.

"Yes, Gerry. As I said before, it is much better to have Camillien on our side. The election is coming up.

I'll be calling it on June 9 for July 28. I need a reliable organizer in Montreal. You know that the Union Nationale lost the urban vote. Most of our support now comes from the countryside. It is dangerous to neglect Montreal. It can backfire on us. The "little guy from Sainte-Marie" could give us the boost that we need. We can't afford not to embrace the political resistance fighter whom Mackenzie King threw into jail in Petawawa. Just think for a minute how we would feel if ever the Liberals decided to court him? I'm about to tour the regions. During that time, Camillien can sell our ideas to "his" Montrealers. I never thought I would need his help so badly. One should never say: "Fountain, I will not drink of thy water"[1].

Duplessis has no intention of missing the opportunity for a reconciliation with his old enemy. Houde, at fifty-nine, is tired and weighed down by the years, and there is no longer any fear of his overshadowing Duplessis. Fifteen years earlier, in 1933, the two men coveted the crown of the leadership of the Conservative Party. Today, the reason for these differences is non-existent. In any case, the reconciliation will benefit both of them. Maurice is sure of it: Camillien Houde, the one whom people call "Mr. Montreal," seeks from the Quebec government a new charter for Montreal, one that would confer more power on him. Ever since Pacifique Plante, a newly appointed assistant in the

1. Refers to one of La Fontaine's fables.

municipal police, has been attempting to eliminate the influence of the mob on public morality, Houde needs to consolidate his power at the municipal level. As for Duplessis, the friendship of the old campaigner will be very useful to the Union Nationale.

"I have planned to hold the last rally of the campaign at the Marché Saint-Jacques in Montreal. I will ask Houde to make one of those speeches that only he knows how to. I'm telling you, Martineau, never in Quebec history will there be such a sweep. We have the wind in our sails. The Union Nationale is young. It is not like the Liberals, an old team dating back to Taschereau's time! The journalists of *Le Devoir*, the guys from La Patente, Gérard Fillion and that pest Pierre Laporte, including the excitable André Laurendeau, they all want to wipe us out. I know they don't like me. But I'm the boss. Yes, the *chef* as they say. As long as I'm the boss, I'll keep my eye on these 'agitators.' The people are not about to elect them on July 28. They're going to elect us!"

∽

With five victories in the by-elections, and satisfied with his government's achievements, Maurice Duplessis throws himself into the campaign, sure of being re-elected as premier of Quebec. A flamboyant political figure, he is very much a character. He has a court of admirers at his beck and call. His MLAs are at his service. When Duplessis rises to take the floor at the Legislative Assembly, Roméo Lorrain, the minister of public works who is seated behind him, and John

Bourque, a member seated to his left, pull back his chair. This mise en scène delights the members of the press gallery, who await the premier's performances like they would those of a stand-up comic. When he wants to silence one of the Opposition members, and even one of his own ministers, he comes out with shocking expressions. Some even claim that he said to Antoine Rivard: "Shut up, you."

In 1948, Duplessis is at the height of his power. He laughs at his opponents. He ridicules the weak and takes on those who oppose him. Duplessis multiplies his verbal attacks with a liberal sprinkling of puns, which Victor Hugo once referred to as the droppings of an airborne mind.

He doesn't deprive himself of the pleasure of shutting up someone he doesn't like. A certain Mr. Thivierge did something Maurice didn't appreciate. Without even thinking, and in front of everyone, he says: "When I look at you, I don't know if you're a *tit vierge* or a *tit crisse*![1]

People burst out laughing. Duplessis, like a peacock, spreads his feathers. He has just scored a goal like his hockey hero Maurice Richard, whose net shots are always on target. Number Nine is the hero of the French Canadians; he is the one who always wins the Stanley Cup for the Canadiens. A winner after Duplessis's own heart. Almost certain of winning the election in July, the leader of the Union Nationale stands out on the political chess board. In Ottawa,

---

1. *Tit vierge* is pronounced like Mr. Thivierge's name. *Vierge*, meaning virgin, is a swear word referring to the Virgin Mary. *Crisse* is the slang for *Christ* and is also a swear word.

Mackenzie King, who has set a record for longevity as head of the Canadian government, will soon pass the torch on to his heir apparent, Louis Saint-Laurent. In Quebec City, Adélard Godbout is not making waves in the Opposition. Rumour has it that he is not even sure of being re-elected in his own riding. As for the Bloc Populaire, time has put an end to their hopes. They will never accede to power and their members are scattered all over the electoral map.

Duplessis, on the other hand, is seen as an authoritarian father figure. He responds to the needs of Quebec society. Even if a few voices, still very timid, are starting to contest the omnipotence of this man who gives himself the airs of a king, he is headed straight for a second coronation.

At Trois-Rivières, where he is starting his whirlwind tour through the regions, Duplessis gets up to speak. Thousands of voters welcome him with cheers. They chant: *"Halte-là, halte-là, halte-là, Maurice est là, Maurice est là."* [Halt. Halt. Maurice is here!] The crowds are delirious when he steps up to the microphone and reminds them of all the promises he has kept in the last four years. Did he not give the province a new flag?

It happened at the beginning of the year. Maurice Duplessis, after a solemn speech in the Legislature, had declared that the Fleur-de-lis from now on would permanently replace the Union Jack. And from that day on, a new Quebec flag flew from the top of the Assembly buildings. "At 3 p.m., on January 21, 1948, I decreed that our province had its own flag. Yes, my dear friends, I am proud to have chosen this official emblem of Quebec and to have offered it to my people!"

Duplessis puffs up: "Three days ago, I had the great honour of inaugurating a bridge that bears my family's name. Building bridges, opening roads – these kinds of projects, among many others, I hold dear to my heart, and my government is very proud of them. Give me another mandate and I will give Quebec its rightful place in Confederation."

In June 1948, while there is growing concern over the blockade of Berlin, which Winston Churchill has called the most serious manifestation of the Cold War, Duplessis launches a new electoral campaign. *In less than a month*, he thinks, *my government will have a new mandate*. Already, in meetings, he speaks as if he were the only possible winner in this race.

9

Down With Unanimity

The day after July 28, 1948, the Union Nationale's victory makes headlines. With 51 per cent of the vote, Duplessis leads with eighty-two members elected. The Liberals have been routed. The re-drawing of the electoral map worked against them. Strong in most urban centres, they have only eight men in the Opposition. And to make matters worse, they no longer have a leader. Adélard Godbout was defeated in his own riding of L'Islet.

Duplessis has every reason to celebrate with his voters. The sweep of the Bleus has consolidated his power and gives him the authority he has always coveted. Seated solidly in the saddle for the next four years, he mounts a spirited horse, ready to rear up

Maurice Duplessis inaugurates a monument in memory
of Thomas Chapais in Rivière-du-Loup.

Maurice Duplessis presides over the benediction
of Jacques Cartier School.

between the shafts of the federal carriage. He now has elbow room to impose the laws that matter deeply to him. "I intend to tackle the Labour Code," he confides. "It is time to clean up this file."

Maurice Duplessis wants to nip in the bud any vague protest coming from the unions. But in actual fact, a series of small strikes darkens his last years in power. The workers in the textile industry are defying management. Recently, the chaos seemed so overwhelming in Valleyfield and Lachute that Duplessis signed an order arresting Madeleine Parent, an activist involved in these strikes. This climate of demands and recriminations is not to the liking of the leader of the government. He is a kind of *père Fouettard*[1] who won't tolerate any disobedience from his children. What is wrong? Why do they want to disobey him? But the postwar economy is booming, and factory workers want their piece of pie.

Canada is now engaged in the process of industrialization and urbanization after coming out of a time of deprivation. Not so long ago families were still using rationing cards to buy a pint of milk or a bag of coal. Today, fancy advertising is wooing the public and offering them a more attractive lifestyle. "Buy a three-thousand-dollar Cadillac," shout the newspaper ads. Workers are tired of tightening their belts. They want salary raises and better working conditions. The surge in the economy should not just benefit the bosses: the low-wage earners also want to benefit.

---

1. A legendary figure who comes on December 5 every year to punish naughty children

Maurice Duplessis won't allow himself to become demoralized. Revived by his electoral victory, he raises his voice against the rebels. Will he be able to contain their discontent much longer?

∞

Situated near the railway station, Chez Gérard has been Quebec City's most popular night club since Charles Trenet performed his most famous songs there. Trenet was known as *Le fou chantant* [the singing fool]. With dancing blue eyes and his hat perched at the back of his head – a felt crown on top of blond curly hair – he charms his audience, who already know by heart the words of *"Douce France"* [Sweet France] and *"Que reste-il de nos amours?"* [What is left of our love?] Maurice is sitting in the back with Gérald Martineau and his wife. He tells them how two years earlier, in June 1947, he had gone to a Maurice Chevalier show at the Palais Montcalm. At the end of the performance, he went backstage to Momo's dressing room to ask him for an autograph.

"I have a photograph of the two of us. Chevalier is quite the showman! You should have seen him sing *Ma pomme*. He danced around imitating a drunk. Trenet is great but he is too nostalgic for me!"

While the audience is applauding, Martineau talks about the last trip he and Maurice took to Ungava Bay. They flew with a group of Americans over the great white desert under which mineral treasures are sleeping.

"There's plenty of iron up there," says Maurice. "My dream is to create a vast steel industry and to increase Quebec's output of hydro-electric power. Jules Timmins told me that he would finance the building of factories. When I hear journalists accuse me of selling the province to rich Americans, it makes me laugh. I'm the premier, and I have no intention of letting these greenhorns tell me what to do. What do they know about prospecting!"

The development of the territories in New Quebec is bound to generate a lot of money for the province and for party coffers. Why hide it? In politics, opportunism is a conjuring trick. Duplessis is already busy converting these iron and titanium deposits into dollars, which is reason enough to announce as soon as possible the opening of mines near the Labrador border. In less than three years, Sept-Îles will be a city with paved streets. Before 1951, it will have its own railroad. The Quebec premier thinks big. The Opposition starts to wonder if he has not borrowed his vision from his friends, those American heavyweights who come here for cheap labour and to export our raw resources.

∞

"Devote! I repeat: you must always use the word *devote* instead of the word *spend*."

Once again, Maurice Duplessis is coaching a minister with a short memory, as to the correct political term to use.

"This year, the Union Nationale will devote twenty million dollars to education. We intend to increase corporate taxes to oblige the federal government to get out of this area. No use explaining everything we plan to do. What counts is to present our projects well. What is particularly important is to avoid giving the impression that we are throwing money out the window."

The Chief leads his troops with authority. "His troops? No... a herd!" quips Pierre Laporte, who is covering the parliamentary debates for *Le Devoir*. His anti-government articles are among the fiercest. He never misses a chance to hound Duplessis and denounce his way of governing and his sickening paternalism. The weakened Opposition is more energetic outside the Assembly than inside. Here and there, islands of resistance are forming. Journalists, union leaders, workers, and intellectuals are mobilizing.

On August 9, 1948, not even two weeks after the Union Nationale's landslide victory, a group of sixteen young artists, led by Paul-Emile Borduas, a longtime professor at the École du meuble [School of Furniture Design], publish an incendiary pamphlet at les éditions Mithra-Mythe of Saint-Hilaire. The title alone is startling: *Le Refus global* [total refusal]. The pamphlet is an anti-religious and anti-establishment manifesto and one of the most influential social and artistic documents in Quebec modern history.

Their shout rends the silence. It is a desperate call for civil and intellectual disobedience, a fifty-page document originating from the depths of despair. Their manifesto, with its surreal aspects, attacks the leaders of a submissive people and proposes a new model of civilization. "Stop using the past to destroy the present and the future." The *Refus global* gives the signal to tear down the existing order.

Who are these passionate young artists? Are some of the signatories readers of the Communist newspaper *Combat*? Do they read Hegel, Marx? *Refus global* is a bomb that must be defused quickly. Maurice Duplessis doesn't even bother trying to understand what he considers a scathing attack. His government isn't about to tolerate any kind of sedition.

On September 4, Borduas is expelled from the École du meuble. Unemployed, he is forced into exile to New York City and eventually settles in Paris. Others also leave. Marcelle Ferron, Fernand Leduc. Quebec will not tolerate anyone who does not walk the straight and narrow. The Promised Land is elsewhere for those suffocating under the dominant ideology.

The intellectuals are able to leave; the workers, on the other hand, are obliged to remain. For years now, their working conditions have been deteriorating. At the end of the Forties, new union leaders are heading up the Confédération des travailleurs catholiques du Canada, the CTCC [Catholic Workers Confederation of Canada]. Gérard Picard becomes president and Jean Marchand, secretary.

The more he hears about them, the more Duplessis hates what they are doing.

"They are downright socialists infected with the ideas of Father Lévesque from Laval University. Dream chasers! They probably can't even add up a grocery bill, and here they are trying to lead the workers!"

His anger explodes in 1949. On February 13, the workers of the Canadian subsidy of the Johns Manville Company in the town of Asbestos go on strike. Their strike is deemed illegal by the premier.

"They'll have to await the mediator's report and undergo arbitration. The law is the law. For everybody. Whether they are right or wrong."

Duplessis is inflexible. No compromise. What do these men want? A wage increase? They average seventy-five cents an hour. They're being offered five cents more. They want fifteen. Moreover, they want to share in the company's profits. But most of all they want improved working conditions. It has been proven that the dust from asbestos mines causes incurable lung diseases. Old miners by the dozen are dying of cancer. They don't even have time to enjoy a well-earned retirement.

The Johns Manville Company is the sole employer in Asbestos, a town of eight thousand inhabitants. The town's name refers to the mineral that is processed into heat-resistant fibers. Eventually, a name is given to the illness that is affecting the striking miners – asbestosis.

Since the founding of this town, every morning hundreds of men – with their helmets, dirty boots, dusty uniforms, and lunch boxes – have disappeared down the mine shafts to extract asbestos. Today, they are on the picket line with their wives and children. They listen to their union leaders harangue them from the stage. Jean Marchand is the fieriest. He has it in for the premier, who is grovelling in front of the millionaire bosses who have more than enough money to give the miners what it is their right to request. This is a fight for dignity, and the battle promises to be a long one.

Maurice Duplessis is furious. The strike drags on. The Johns Manville Company hires scabs, but nothing changes. The strikebreakers are having a hard time of it. In a village where everyone knows everyone else, the traitors are being singled out. The neighbours heckle them. They take their revenge by breaking the windows of the strikebreakers' homes. The government is worried. Day after day, the conflict hardens. It becomes like a flame ready to spread, ready to burst into wildfire and inflame those who are still lukewarm. The workers aren't the only ones involved in the fight. Several factions who oppose the government have joined in the union's revolt.

"What? Monsignor Joseph Charbonneau is organizing a food drive for the strikers? Now even the bishop of Montreal is getting mixed up in politics?"

The news hits home. What a blow for Duplessis, who has never really liked Charbonneau. If the Church is now on the side of the workers, the world has turned upside down! Quick, the strike has to end in Asbestos; otherwise, the social contract could start to collapse.

May 4, 1949, is a decisive date. The strikers have run out of patience. They rebel. Violence breaks out. The agitation of the first few weeks is giving way to rage. How far will the strikers go? After discussions with his closest advisers, Duplessis calls in the provincial police.

On the morning of May 5, convoys roll into the seething town. Judge O'Bready arrives, accompanied by the forces of the law. The news spreads like wildfire. The people of Asbestos gather by the hundreds in front of the parish church of Saint-Aimé. Speaking in a loud and solemn voice, the judge reads out the Riot Act, which can condemn a striker to life imprisonment if he refuses to go home peacefully. Violence breaks out.

Some 180 arrests are made. The miners of Asbestos are coerced into capitulation, under pain of severe sanctions.

Duplessis has won. He has succeeded in putting down what had become a veritable insurrection. Now he must find a solution to the labour dispute. After lengthy arbitration, the CTCC signs an agreement in July.

The Asbestos strike marks a major change in Duplessis's political life. Without being fully aware of it at the time, he has written a page of Quebec history. The lovely unanimity of the old days has been wrecked. On the one hand, there are those sworn to support Duplessis's government. They are known as the *Duplessistes*. On the other hand, there are those dissatisfied with the government who do not fear controversy. For them, the premier is a only a puppet dictator.

In 1950, Gérard Pelletier, a clear-eyed critic of the events surrounding the Asbestos strike, and Pierre Elliott Trudeau, an activist who supported his friend Jean Marchand in Asbestos, start up a magazine called *Cité libre*. The title reflects an ideal. The magazine becomes a forum for Duplessis's adversaries, a stone thrown into the pond of the dominant ideology. Every article is a slap in the face of the one who holds the reins in Quebec. Duplessis is not upset by the language used in this new protest magazine. He is persuaded that he has taken back control of his province. And, in any case, he has other things on his plate.

Msgr. Charbonneau has gone too far, he says to himself. *Maybe he should be given a lesson in humility.*

∞

Gérald Martineau, in response to a journalist who has been hot on his heels for weeks, says that Maurice Duplessis had nothing to do with the resignation of the archbishop of Montreal.

"You are aware that Msgr. Joseph Charbonneau's health no longer permits him to carry out his functions. If he's left for British Columbia, it's because he has friends there. In any case, all that is over now. Our new archbishop, Msgr. Paul-Émile Léger, does his work very well, and we continue to carry on with our own projects. Speaking of which, you can tell your friends who are covering the inauguration of the new highway to come and see me at the end of the ceremony. I will be at a table at the back of the parish hall. I have an envelope for each one of them…"

"How much in each envelope?"

"As always – a nice little fifty."

"You're not afraid what people will say, that Duplessis is trying to buy us? That everyone knows he can't stand criticism. That he always wants us to say that he's doing good work!"

Martineau is hardly surprised. Politics is a game with no rules. And so what if some small-time journalist is acting shocked. The Union Nationale has succeeded in staying in power because its leader has more than one trick up his sleeve. A good article in the newspaper is worth its price.

"Listen to me, young fellow, you take Maurice Duplessis's envelopes without asking any questions. Or we'll ask the editor-in-chief to relegate you to the women's pages!"

In his free time, Maurice likes to drive to Boischâtel, on the Beaupré Coast, to spend the evening with Father Pierre Gravel, an old acquaintance with whom he enjoys discussing current affairs. They have a great time tearing the Liberals apart. Duplessis keeps casting back to the Opposition's behaviour when the Trois-Rivières Bridge collapsed. The accident caused four deaths.

"Lapalme's MLAs didn't even offer their condolences to the grief-stricken families."

Then he murmurs: "My bridges aren't standing up. It is bad for my image."

Duplessis doesn't like the current political climate. He has too many enemies and he is feeling exhausted. But he still intends to call an election because, in all probability, the Union Nationale would win. Quebec is enjoying a period of prosperity, which works to the government's advantage and gives people the impression that it alone is responsible for this growth.

The Fifties see the birth of the age of consumerism. The United States, under President Eisenhower, is leading the free countries against the Soviet Union, which, just before Stalin's death in March 1953, extended its hegemony beyond Russia's borders. In Canada, a shiny new capitalism is blossoming. Young people are dancing to rock and roll. Soon, Elvis Presley will sell millions of 45 rpm records, and his songs will top the hit parades. In Quebec, everyone is talking about buying a new appliance – a television like those advertised by Dupuis Frères in *La Presse*. In

September, Radio-Canada will launch its first French-language television station. But Duplessis is not keen on appearing before the cameras.

"I've always had a weak spot for radio. And I don't trust the people who work at Radio-Canada. They're the type who read *Le Devoir*, and you know my opinion of that newspaper! Did you know that Msgr. Charbonneau was a shareholder of this paper? That's why I'm not surprised to see so many libellous articles about me. Gérard Pelletier, Gérard Filion, and that other little journalist nipping at my heels, Pierre Laporte, are all trying to corner me. They would like to see me mixed up in scandals. Laporte is fierce in his pursuit. I wouldn't be surprised to see him get into politics, that one."

Duplessis recounts how, in April 1945, he sanctioned a law authorizing the creation of a provincial radio-broadcasting service. "It would have been called Radio-Québec, but it didn't get off the ground," he says without bitterness. But he is proud of having acquired *Montréal-Matin*, a modern newspaper with lots of photos, which concentrates on sensationalism and sports. The newspaper, a member of United Press, is doing well.

"Everyone knows that the Union Nationale is behind Jacques Francoeur's tabloid! I am often on the front page. It is good for the party. The journalists of *Montréal-Matin* are able to silence the wagging tongues of *Le Devoir*."

As head of a government that has been in power for almost fifteen years, Maurice Duplessis needs the media just to stay in place. He is wary of television. He doesn't like seeing photographs of himself. And the cartoonists have a field day with him. Normand Hudon and Robert Lapalme, among others, draw him with a pointy nose, a sour mouth, a moustache like a broom, and a weasel's eyes. Over time, the head of the Union Nationale has become their whipping boy.

"I forgive them," he says into the microphone before a gathering of supporters. "And I hope they'll forget their insults because otherwise they'll have to live with their regrets!" Duplessis is annoyed by these new adversaries, who take up a lot of space. He is aware of his charisma when he speaks directly to the crowd. But television transmits an image of him that he cannot control. The screen magnifies his faults, warps his stature.

"The press is my most faithful ally and my best friends are the English: John McConnell at the head of the *Montreal Star* and John Bassett at the *Gazette*. And there is always Abel Vineberg, who covers parliamentary life in Quebec City and whom I have known since 1927."

His friend Gravel interrupts him:

"Vineberg, your lay confessor, as Pierre Laporte calls him."

"That is malicious gossip from people who like to laugh at me. He laughs longest who laughs last. The election is coming up. *Le Devoir*, *Cité libre*, *La Presse*, Radio-Canada, all the Quebec intellectuals, the real ones, the false ones, they can rant and rave against me and my team, but the Bleus will crack open the champagne on July 16, 1952. We'll knock them for a loop like Rocky Marciano did when he had Joe Louis on the ropes last year. Pierre, come and drink a toast with us. It'll be quite a party!"

∞

Since the end of the Taschereau régime, whose downfall Duplessis helped bring about, the Liberal Opposition has had trouble recovering. For a while, thanks to Adélard Godbout, the Rouges thought they were strong enough to fight the Union Nationale. But the big Bleu machine functions like a bulldozer. It flattens everything in its path. Its secret lies in its strong connection with the grassroots nurtured by the small organizers working in the ridings.

"Duplessis buys his voters." The battle cry is launched. Stories circulate about the system of telegrams. The Union Nationale is reputed to be paying supporters to vote more than once. Even the dead are resurrected! In fact in Beauce, there were more votes than voters. The premier does not react. How does one reply to skeptics?

"My dear friends, it is the mark of the people's enthusiasm for the Bleus!"

When Duplessis's men are accused of political patronage, he counterattacks. According to him, it is proper to thank those who support his party. If a contractor wants to build a road and needs subsidies, is it not normal for the Union Nationale to request in return that he support the Party? "The businessman needs us as much as we need him. There's nothing wrong with that!"

The Liberals don't stand a chance against Duplessis. Since Adélard Godbout's defeat in 1948, George Marler, an English notary and member from Westmount, is the acting leader of the Opposition.

Despite his distinguished bearing, he can't measure up to Duplessis. In the early Fifties, the Liberal Party decides that they have to find another leader. Georges-Émile Lapalme, former MP with the federal government, is named head of the Liberal MLAs.

"I'm not afraid of Lapalme" says Duplessis, "even if Louis Saint-Laurent and all of Ottawa support him."

Maurice is wrong to dismiss his new adversary so lightly. Lapalme does have the stuff of a leader even if he is very discreet. On July 26, not surprisingly, the Union Nationale is once again returned to power, but with a diminished majority. With little more than half the votes, Maurice Duplessis's party won almost three-quarters of the seats at the Legislative Assembly. However, they lost fifteen seats compared to 1948 and gained only one new one.

Duplessis meets his friends to analyse his victory, which he owes mainly to the way the electoral map is drawn up. Also, his use of sensationalist tactics helped him maintain power by creating a climate of fear among the undecided. In 1952, speaking to the Trifluvians[1] from his fiefdom of Trois-Rivières, Duplessis has a resounding message for his electors:

"We have sixty-eight seats against twenty-eight for the Liberals. I've always thought that the people in the rural ridings were our most faithful allies. Today I have the proof. Believe me, I am not about to forget your loyalty. The Union Nationale is your party. And I will prove it to you over the next four years!"

Duplessis is hailed triumphantly. He rejoices in

---

1. People of Trois-Rivières.

his victory because since early 1952, his health has been deteriorating. In February, he is hospitalized for a diabetic attack. "I thought I would have to campaign from my hospital bed," he confides to the journalists. As soon as his convalescence is over, he starts travelling all over the province to promote his party's program. In the early Fifties, his projects include an improved infrastructure for the province, a new Department of Transport, and renewed efforts to reclaim more fiscal power from Ottawa .

At the federal-provincial conferences held almost annually during Maurice Duplessis's last four mandates, the leader of the Quebec government takes on the role of defender of the autonomist cause. He feels strongly that to govern a province you have to have the power to tax. It is time to take back control of the Quebec economy.

Speaking from this perspective, Maurice Duplessis puts forward an idea considered very anti-Canadian at the time: a provincial tax. This change to the personal income tax law, which comes into force in 1954, is his way of ensuring substantial new revenues for the Quebec government. The action forces the federal government to reduce their own taxes by 10 per cent. After long and arduous constitutional battles, the premier of Quebec finds himself, in the mid-1950s, stronger than ever. The political situation in Canada plays in his favour. Louis Saint-Laurent, whom Duplessis respects, is at the end of a long career that began in 1921 with Mackenzie King.

"Uncle Louis wears his surname well," confides Maurice to his ministers. "He is a wise man whom nobody fears. But he's at the end of his rope. The Conservative Party is impatient to take power on Parliament Hill. If ever John Diefenbaker is elected – a unilingual Anglo from the West! – Quebec will have no more say in the Confederation."

Duplessis realizes that if he wants to squeeze something out of the federal government, he has to act quickly. All the more so since destabilizing strikes are breaking out all over the province. In May 1952, the employees of the Dupuis Frères department store walk out and demonstrate in the streets of Montreal to demand higher wages. During the annual St-Jean-Baptiste parade, the more fiery marchers pelt Camillien Houde with whatever is handy as he waves to the crowds.

The political climate is rife with protest. In Louiseville, the strike in the textile industry, which started over the right to unionize, harks back to the Asbestos strike of 1949. Duplessis, once again, resorts to force and calls in the police. Defeated, the workers return to work, but the union leaders, who confess to leading their troops in what they knew would be a futile strike, are determined to launch other battles against a weary government. The outcome of the textile workers' strike has everything to please the premier. As far as he is concerned, it is up to the State to impose order at the risk of using unfair police repression. Management must be reassured. And Duplessis, once again, reiterates his mantra: "We have the resources, they have the money."

. But Duplessis's government is running out of energy. In 1956, the victory of the Bleus is due in part to the support of the regional ridings and in part to the weakness of Georges-Émile Lapalme's Liberals. Physically diminished, Duplessis has trouble controlling those around him. However, he is not perturbed by the natural gas scandal of 1957. Eight of his ministers are accused of pocketing illicit profits from the sale of the public provider of natural gas to private industry. He defends himself by claiming that his government is always at the service of the people – despite the occasional swerve off the road. He hammers away at the people with hard-hitting words: "The Union Nationale is there to set the table, prepare the food, cook it, put it into your mouths, but you must at least swallow what you are fed!"

Today, Maurice Duplessis is spending the evening with his friend, John W. McConnell, owner of the *Montreal Star*, in his richly furnished home on Pine Avenue. For his sixty-eighth birthday last year, the magnate gave Maurice a twenty-dollar gold coin dating back to 1890, the year of Duplessis's birth. The premier always enjoys discussing his projects with this businessman who wields considerable influence in the English-speaking community. In financial circles, they are worried. The government of the Union Nationale is being challenged. Last year, for example, university students demanded more money to improve their living conditions.

"The three students known as the group *Trois de Québec* [Three from Quebec] even came to my office," says Maurice, who cannot hide his anger. "I kept them waiting for thirty-seven days! I won't be ordered around by kids who are still wearing out the seat of their pants on school benches!"

Duplessis senses that time has eroded some of his power.

"Luckily," he continues, "I always keep my eye on the public sector of the province. The hospitals and the schools are in the hands of the religious orders, whom I trust completely. I believe in the partnership of State and Church as I recently said in an interview with *Le Devoir*. Religion is necessary for an educational system to work well. Even if I did refuse the federal subsidy for education, I accepted money from Ottawa for Mont-Providence."

Duplessis recounts how he recently signed an order-in-council changing the mission of this institution. Does it really matter that from now on these orphans will be considered mentally ill? The administrators and the doctors have only to fill out their forms, and Mont-Providence will receive the subsidy it has been requesting for so long.

"In a way" says McConnell," these abandoned children will now be your orphans! You know, Maurice, some of your enemies are not pleased. They accuse you of religious capitalism. To see you in action, you are like the head of a spiritual and temporal state. Pope and Premier!"

"Don't forget that the bishops eat out of my hand," retorts Duplessis.

"Cardinal Paul-Émile Léger is more reticent than the archbishop of Quebec, Maurice Roy," comments McConnell.

"I often say: I prefer a Monsignor Roy to a Cardinal Léger!"

Duplessis smirks behind his cigar smoke. Raised to the rank of cardinal by Pope Pius XII, Paul-Émile Léger is an impressive spokesman who involves himself in the Unioniste government's decisions regarding social policy. Maurice remembers Léger's return from Rome when the crowds welcomed him at the railway station.

"Do you know what he said? 'Montreal, my beloved city, you make yourself beautiful to welcome back your Prince!' When I compare myself to Cardinal Léger, I feel pretty modest."

John McConnell prefers not to comment. What interests him are the government's upcoming projects. Is it true that Schefferville now has a population of two thousand and that the Hollinger Company and its subsidiary, the Iron Ore Company, intend to continue investing in the area?

"Are you planning a trip up north?" he asks Duplessis.

"Yes. I'm going in September even though my diabetes is acting up. J.H. Thompson, president of Iron Ore, is coming up from Cleveland. He will join Jules Timmins, Martineau, and myself. To tell you the truth, I don't really feel like going. Flying tires me. We'll stay in a company house, a chalet on a peninsula overlooking Lake Knob. I'm anxious to be back. My agenda is full until the end of September."

Duplessis takes his agenda out of his pocket and reels off his engagements.

"On September 7th, I'm inaugurating a plaque in a Trois-Rivières park in honour of Ezechiel Hart, the first Jewish MLA of Lower Canada. On the 8th, I'll be in Quebec City for a banquet. On the 13th, in Granby. On the 14th, back in Quebec City for a banquet of the Bar Association."

"Don't forget the by-elections on September 16 in Labelle and Lac-Saint-Jean," says McConnell. "My journalists will be there. You have a good chance of winning."

"My dear John, next year, around July 1960, I will undertake my ninth electoral campaign and I intend to be back for another mandate, at the head of a majority Unioniste government. But until then, I have a lot on my plate. September is going to be one of the busiest months. Let's meet in October and I'll tell you about my trip to Sept-Îles with Thompson."

10

The End of an Era

On a Tuesday in early September, the day before his departure for the Côte-Nord, Maurice Duplessis convenes his cabinet. They discuss subsidies to various companies and institutions. Duplessis confides to his ministers that he is anxious to be back in the Legislature. What he likes best about his life as a politician are the debates, the unpredictable confrontations between himself and the Opposition. For some time now, his health has forced him to slow down. He even looks different. His cheeks are sunken. He has aged a lot in the last few months. His doctor, Dr. Lucien Larue at Saint-Michel-Archange Hospital in Quebec City, has warned him that if he doesn't change his lifestyle immediately, he won't last the year.

Maurice Duplessis died on September 7, 1959.

"Rest," he ordered the premier. If he were wise, Maurice would step down. This would also give his MLAs the opportunity to test their chances in the battle for the leadership of the Union Nationale before the election. But Maurice is adamant: there is no way he will retire before the end of his mandate. He would prefer to die in the trenches rather than withdraw from the battle.

On the runway at the Quebec City airport, shadows darken the fog of a nippy autumn morning. Seven passengers hurry to catch the plane, which is taking off at 10 a.m. Once on board, the passengers settle down for the trip to Sept-Îles. Travelling with the premier are Jules Timmins and J. H. Thompson, directors of Iron Ore, Gérald Martineau, Maurice Custeau, and Gérald Thibault, members of the Unioniste caucus, and Jacques Bureau, Duplessis's nephew. Maurice, who got up as usual at 6 a.m., took the time to go to the Basilica to pray. Duplessis reassures Martineau, who is worried about his health. "Everything is fine. Yesterday, I phoned my friend Father Gravel and asked him to send me good thoughts. I'm anxious to see the Côte-Nord..."

At noon, the plane lands smoothly on a snowy runway. An open limousine is waiting to take Duplessis on the official tour of the town founded less than ten years ago.

"This is the realization of one of my fondest dreams," he says to the crowds come to acclaim him. "The towns of the Côte-Nord are extending Quebec's horizons. In 1927, Newfoundland stole Labrador from us. But our territory has never been so vast."

Duplessis congratulates the crowds for their courage. The future lies in these families willing to exile themselves and found parishes just like the settlers did in the 1800s in the Pays-d'en-Haut. He singles out Curé Labelle in Saint-Jérôme, and Msgr. Labrie on the Côte-Nord. For Duplessis, the Catholic Church must remain the sole guardian of social values.

On September 3, accompanied by his fellow travellers, Maurice flies to Schefferville, five hundred kilometres north of Sept-Îles. If there is a town that Duplessis really loves, it is this municipality that owes its name to Msgr. Lionel Scheffer, the first bishop of Labrador-Schefferville. Duplessis knew the Monsignor before he went to live in Blanc-Sablon in 1946. Appointed apostolic vicar of Labrador, Msgr. Scheffer often visits the premier in Quebec City. Neither the Department of Colonization nor the Public Health Department would ever refuse Msgr. Scheffer anything. Duplessis has even given out of his own pocket to support the prelate's humanitarian works. In September 1959, he is happy to see his old friend again – another excellent reason to venture into this wild region that has long been called the Land of Cain.

"If you have a hospital here and roads, it is because of us, the Unionistes," says Mr. Duplessis as he walks towards the pavilion of the Iron Ore Company.

Before returning to Quebec City, some of the party plan to go salmon fishing on Lake Knob, where the chalet is situated. Maurice is not feeling up to it. His friends invite him to come along but he refuses. "I prefer to stay by the fire."

He is not alone. Maurice Custeau keeps him company, while Gérald Martineau goes off for a nap.

It is a little past noon when the fishermen hear a shout coming from the chalet.

"Quick, come quickly, Maurice has had a diabetic attack."

A director of the mine calls a doctor. While the sick man is being moved to the sofa, Dr. Horst Rosmus, the only doctor in Schefferville, rushes to his side. A very agitated Martineau wants to be reassured.

"Mr. Duplessis felt faint. He is alive, see how he clenches his right fist...," says Martineau.

Dr. Rosmus takes Duplessis's pulse, and examines him.

"I regret to have to tell you that it is very serious," says Rosmus. "A cerebral hemorrhage."

Martineau refuses to accept this diagnosis. He jumps up and accuses Rosmus of being a bad doctor. "Quickly," he says to his friends, "we need to call another doctor."

"Dr. Lucien Larue knows him best," says Martineau. "He works at the Saint-Michel-Archange hospital. I'll phone him and ask him to come. In the meantime, get a priest to administer the last rites."

Towards the end of the afternoon, a plane lands in Schefferville, bringing Doctors Larue and Rouleau, accompanied by nurses. They run to the car, which pulls away quickly. At the Lake Knob chalet, short of breath, his face contorted in pain, the premier has suffered three more attacks. Father Champagne is at his side. For several hours now, the priest has been murmuring the prayer for the dying. Duplessis's travelling companions, who had stayed back in Schefferville, are gathered around the bed, praying. Étiennette Bureau, Duplessis's sister, who left Trois-Rivières in a mad panic earlier that day, is also there. She speaks into his ear, trying to awaken him:

"We'll take you back to the house," she says. "We'll look after you, Maurice. You'll get better."

As the last rites are being administered, Martineau approaches his old friend, and taking the premier's hand, he finds himself using the formal *vous*:

"Maurice, Maurice, say: 'Bon Jésus, Miséricorde'!"

Maurice is not sick. He is dying.

The diagnosis of Doctors Larue and Bouleau is harsh: the premier does not have very long to live. At most, a few days. Taking Martineau aside, Larue says to him:

"It all depends on his resistance. He is solid, he can still fight."

Maurice Duplessis suffers from hypospadia – a malformation of the penis in which the urethra opens on the under surface – which makes it very difficult to take urine samples. Dr. Larue says that Dr. Rosmus, with whom Martineau had lost his temper this morning, did his best. He could not have saved him.

Maurice Duplessis dies a little after midnight on September 7, 1959, Labour Day. There are no caskets in Schefferville. One is sent from Quebec City. John W. McConnell orders the most expensive casket from the Canadian Casket Company at a cost of 8700 dollars. As is the custom, a member of the Union Nationale, Maurice Cloutier, looks after the arrangements. Despite Gérald Martineau's instructions, news of the premier's death does not remain secret very long. At dawn, journalists start arriving in this remote town of the Côte-Nord. Those who remain in the chalet are nervous and wonder what to do.

"Where can we find a Quebec flag to put on Mr. Duplessis's coffin?" asks the ever faithful and farsighted Martineau.

The mayor is able to dig one up at the Schefferville school commission. They have to hurry. Reporters have started to storm the Lake Knob chalet. Armed with cameras, the bolder ones have succeeded in reaching the windows in the hope of immortalizing a last image of Duplessis. But to no avail. In the morning, the coffin, under police protection, is transported by car to the airport. During this time, in Quebec City, ministers and MLAs of the Union Nationale are reminiscing about Duplessis's famous quips. One of them recalls the visit of Pierre Mendès France to Quebec. Duplessis, wishing to make fun of the political instability in France at the time, had asked his guest how long he had been sitting in his office.

"I don't know," stammered Mendès France, without fully understanding the question, "maybe twenty minutes?"

Duplessis had retorted rather insolently:

"Are you sure that your country has not changed government since you've been here?"

A Member points out that Maurice Duplessis has been the longest reigning premier in the history of Quebec. He has occupied this public position for eighteen years, fifteen of which were consecutive.

"Maurice wouldn't have wanted us to be sad," he said. "He died while he was still in office. Many owe him a lot. He was more than a leader of a party, he was a father to us."

∞

Maurice Duplessis's remains are laid out in state in the Legislative Assembly where he sat for almost thirty years, in the building that he considered his second home. More than 100,000 people come to pay their respects. The mourners cross themselves and pray in front of the open coffin. Sadness overcomes the people paying homage for the last time. On the morning of September 11, the hearse, followed by a procession of fifty flower cars, heads for Trois-Rivières to the cathedral, where the state funeral, both grandiose and unique, is officiated by Cardinal Paul-Émile Léger and Msgr. Maurice Roy.

On the front pages of all the newspapers, those who knew him well remember the premier of Quebec. Those who had loved him, those who had fought him, all pay moving tribute to him. Later, there will be time enough to look over the balance sheet of his long political reign. For the time being, death imposes a truce.

"A colossus has fallen," George-Émile Lapalme and Jean Lesage say. André Laurendeau points out Duplessis's courage. "He went down fighting," he concludes. Television, which is only seven years old, creates an event out of the mourning. For the first time, Quebecers are able to follow the funeral of a celebrity on the screen. They are like guests attending an official ceremony, like members of a big family mourning the loss of one of theirs.

With Duplessis's death, a new era begins. "From now on…" is the motto of his successor, Paul Sauvé, who dies prematurely on January 2, 1960 after only one hundred days in office. Under the leadership of Antonio Barrette, the Union Nationale goes into decline. On June 22, 1960, Jean Lesage's Liberal Party wins a victory. It is the start of the *Révolution tranquille*, the Quiet Revolution.

Maurice Duplessis, the bon vivant,
in his time a familiar face in Quebec.

Chronology of Maurice Duplessis (1890-1959)

Compiled by Michèle Vanasse

MAURICE DUPLESSIS AND QUEBEC	CANADA AND THE WORLD

1886

Nérée Duplessis is elected Conservative member of the Quebec legislature for the riding of Saint-Maurice.

Honoré Mercier, Leader of the National Party – an amalgam of Liberals and disaffected Conservatives – wins the provincial election by a slim margin. Mercier becomes premier in January of 1887.

1890

Maurice Le Noblet Duplessis is born on April 20 in Trois-Rivières, the son of Nérée Duplessis and Berthe Genest. He has four sisters: Marguerite, Jeanne, Étienette, and Gabrielle.

1885

A new transcontinental railway, the Canadian Pacific Railway, is completed.

The Statue of Liberty in New York commemorates the friendship between France and the United States (U.S.).

1890

In the U.S., the Battle of Wounded Knee in South Dakota brings defeat to the Sioux under Chief Big Foot. The American cavalry win the conflict.

MAURICE DUPLESSIS AND QUEBEC	**CANADA AND THE WORLD**
1896	**1896**
Conservative Edmund James Flynn becomes premier.	Wilfrid Laurier, a Liberal, becomes Canada's first prime minister of French ancestry.
1897	**1897**
Félix-Gabriel Marchand, leader of the Liberals, becomes premier. Nérée Duplessis is re-elected, but finds himself in the Opposition.	In Great Britain, Dr. Guglielmo Marconi establishes the first wireless telegraphic contact. Joseph John Thomson discovers the presence of electrons in the atom.
1898	**1898**
Maurice Duplessis enters Notre-Dame College in Montreal as a boarder. He is a good student. He meets Brother André, who becomes his friend.	The U.S. Army intervenes in the war between Spain and Cuba. Cuba becomes independent under U.S. protection. This signals the end of Spanish hegemony in the Americas.
Monsignor Laflèche dies. He was a friend of the Duplessis family and a proponent of the ultramontane ideology that holds the Church supreme above the State.	The U.S. annexes Hawaii, a U.S. protectorate.
	In France, Pierre and Marie Curie discover Radium.
1900	**1900**
The Liberal Simon Napoléon Parent is elected premier.	Paris hosts the World's Fair. Films by Louis Lumière and Georges Méliès are projected onto a giant screen.
1901	**1901**
The Northern Aluminum Co. opens the first Canadian aluminum smelter in Shawinigan.	In the U.S., Theodore Roosevelt becomes president after the assassination of President William McKinley.

MAURICE DUPLESSIS AND QUEBEC

CANADA AND THE WORLD

In Great Britain, Queen Victoria dies and Edward VII ascends to the throne.

1903

At age 13, Duplessis enters the Seminary at Trois-Rivières to complete his studies in Classics.

Olivar Asselin founds the Ligue nationaliste [Nationalist League]. Lionel Groulx and Émile Chartier, both priests, start the Association catholique de la jeunesse canadienne-française [association of French-Canadian Catholic youth leagues] (ACJC). These youth movements demand greater autonomy for Canada, which is still under British rule.

The Liberal Party of Quebec starts publication of a new newspaper, *Le Canada*.

1905

Lomer Gouin, a Liberal, becomes premier.

1903

In Canada, the Grand Trunk Co. builds a new transcontinental railway.

In the U.S., Henry Ford founds the Ford Motor Co. The Wright brothers complete the first airplane flight since Clément Ader, a French inventor and flight pioneer, made a short flight in 1890.

With U.S. help, Panama becomes independent from Colombia. The U.S. claims the right to build, administer and safeguard the Panama Canal.

1905

The provinces of Alberta and Saskatchewan join the Canadian Confederation.

Albert Einstein publishes his paper on the *Special Theory of Relativity*, revolutionizing modern physics.

1907

In Canada, the luxurious Ouimetoscope, the world's first theatre exclusively for movies, opens on Sainte-Catherine Street in Montreal. Built by Ernest Ouimet,

MAURICE DUPLESSIS AND QUEBEC	CANADA AND THE WORLD

the theatre has 1200 seats and air conditioning.

1908

Duplessis enters the Faculty of Law at the Université de Laval at Montreal.

A raging fire destroys part of Trois-Rivières.

1908

In France and Great Britain, the Suffragette movement demands the vote for women.

In the U.S., the General Motors Company is founded.

1910

Nationalist Henri Bourassa founds the newspaper *Le Devoir*.

The first settlers move north to colonize the Abitibi region.

1910

Parliament passes the Naval Law, creating the Canadian Navy. Prime Minister Wilfrid Laurier proposes free trade with the U.S.

In Great Britain, George V succeeds Edward VII.

1912

The Liberals under Lomer Gouin are re-elected.

The Ungava region comes under Quebec jurisdiction.

1912

Woodrow Wilson becomes president of the U.S.

The *Titanic*, the world's largest passenger liner, sinks off the coast of Newfoundland.

1913

Duplessis is admitted to the Bar. He sets up his practice in Trois-Rivières.

Father Papin Archambault establishes the Ligue des droits du français [league for French language rights].

1913

The young lawyer Mahatma Gandhi starts his campaign for India's independence, based on principles of non-violence.

MAURICE DUPLESSIS
AND QUEBEC

CANADA AND THE WORLD

1914
The First World War breaks out. Austria and Germany are allied against Russia, France, and Great Britain.

The Canadian Parliament votes to enter the war on the side of Great Britain.

1917
Quebec strongly opposes conscription. The conscription crisis threatens Canadian unity.

L'Action française, a monthly magazine, is started by the Ligue des droits du français.

1917
The U.S. enters the war on the side of the Allies.

In Russia, the February revolution results in the abdication of Tsar Nicholas II in March. Lenin and his Bolshevist forces take power in October and negotiate a separate peace under the Brest-Litovsk Treaty with Germany.

1918
Canadian women receive the right to vote.

The First World War ends. The armistice is signed on November 11, 1918.

1919
Canon Lionel Groulx publishes *La Naissance d'une race* [Birth of a Race], and Father Marie-Victorin *Récits laurentiens* [Laurentian Stories].

The Université de Montréal frees itself from the administrative arm

1919
Prohibition (against alcohol) is declared in the U.S.

The Treaty of Versailles redraws the borders of Central Europe and the Balkans.

U.S. President Wilson's dream becomes true when the League of

MAURICE DUPLESSIS AND QUEBEC	CANADA AND THE WORLD
of Université de Laval in Quebec City.	Nations is created to assure future collective security. The League's headquarters is located in Geneva.

1920
Louis-Alexandre Taschereau is elected Liberal premier.

Canon Lionel Groulx takes on the leadership of *L'Action française*.

1920
Arthur Meighen becomes prime minister of Canada, replacing Robert Borden.

In the U.S., women receive the right to vote.

1921
The CTCC, the Confédération des travailleurs catholiques du Canada [Catholic Workers Confederation of Canada] is founded. In 1960, the CTCC becomes the Confederation of National Trade Unions (CNTU).

The Legislative Assembly adopts the Quebec Public Charges Act. The Liquor Board is created, later to be renamed the Société des alcohols du Québec (SAQ).

1921
Liberal Mackenzie King is elected prime minister of Canada.

Ireland is divided into two autonomous territories: the Irish Free State (Catholic), a dominion, and Northern Ireland (Protestant), a division of the United Kingdom of Great Britain.

China turns Communist. Mao Zedong is one of the founders of the Chinese Communist Party.

1922
A law is adopted for the Preservation of Historic and Artistic Monuments to protect Quebec's heritage. The Public Hygiene Act also receives assent.

The Federated Co-operative of Quebec is created.

1922

The Congress of Soviets founds the Union of Soviet Socialist Republics (U.S.S.R.). Joseph Stalin is elected secretary general of the Bolshevist Party.

1923
Louis-Alexandre Taschereau is re-elected as premier.

1923
Mustafa Kemal Atatürk declares Turkey a republic.

MAURICE DUPLESSIS AND QUEBEC

Maurice Duplessis, a first-time candidate, loses his first bid for office in Trois-Rivières. Camillien Houde is one of the newly elected Conservatives.

1927
Louis-Alexandre Taschereau is re-elected as premier.

Maurice Duplessis wins his first election and becomes the Conservative member for Trois-Rivières.

1928
Camillien Houde becomes mayor of Montreal for the first time. He is also re-elected as a member of the Quebec legislature in a by-election.

1929
In July, Camillien Houde succeeds Arthur Sauvé as leader of the Conservative Party of Quebec. But despite his efforts, Conservatives lose four by-elections.

In September, Duplessis has a severe car accident. He is drinking heavily.

1930
Duplessis is ill and remains bedridden for several months.

CANADA AND THE WORLD

1927
The Privy Council of Great Britain makes Labrador part of Newfoundland.

Charles Lindbergh is the first to cross the Atlantic non-stop from New York to Paris: 5,800 km in 33 hours and 30 minutes.

Ho Chi Minh founds the Communist Party of Vietnam.

1928
In Paris, the Kellogg-Briand Pact, a multinational treaty to outlaw war as a means of settling international disputes, is signed.

1929
On Black Thursday, October 24, the U.S. stock exchange collapses. Frantic speculation and easy access to credit lead to panic, which causes a precipitous drop in production. The ten-year-long Great Depression begins.

1930
Conservative R.B. Bennett becomes prime minister of Canada.

Maurice Duplessis

MAURICE DUPLESSIS AND QUEBEC

CANADA AND THE WORLD

The Unemployment Act, which clears the way for certain public works projects to help the unemployed, is ratified.

France begins the construction of the Maginot Line, a string of fortifications connected by underground tunnels, intended to defend Alsace and Lorraine.

1931
Taschereau's Liberals win the election.

Maurice Duplessis, re-elected in the riding of Trois-Rivières, leads Conservative dissidents who refuse to accept a vote recount. They fear the loss of their seats.

The Jeunesse ouvrière catholique [young Catholic workers] is founded and provision is made to grant direct aid to the poor.

1931
The Westminster Statute confirms the independence of Canada from Great Britain, both nationally and internationally.

1933
Maurice Duplessis becomes leader of the Conservative Party of Quebec.

Jean-Marie Rodrigue Villeneuve, archbishop of Quebec, is named cardinal.

The Report on Social Assistance Insurance in Quebec is published.

1933
A year after he is elected president of the U.S., Franklin Delano Roosevelt starts implementing the New Deal, an economic and social program designed to alleviate the effects of unemployment caused by the Great Depression.

Adolf Hitler becomes chancellor of Germany.

1934
The Action libérale nationale [national liberal action group] is founded under the leadership of Paul Gouin, son of Lomer Gouin and grandson of Honoré Mercier. He advocates a program of social

1934
Mao Zedong begins the Long March at the head of the Chinese Communist army. He aims to garner the support of the masses and start a peasant rather than a proletarian revolution in China.

MAURICE DUPLESSIS
AND QUEBEC

renewal called the Programme de restauration sociale, which was published in 1933 and groups together the various nationalist movements in Quebec.

Adrien Arcand founds an extreme right-wing party, the Parti national social chrétien [Christian National Socialist Party].

1935
On the eve of the election, Maurice Duplessis merges his Conservative Party with Paul Gouin's Action Libérale Nationale. Taschereau's Liberals win with a slim majority of six seats.

1936
The Public Accounts Committee, convened by Duplessis, exposes the corruption in the Taschereau government. Taschereau is replaced by Adélard Godbout, who calls a new election.

Maurice Duplessis, now head of the newly named Union Nationale party, wins the election.

Brother Marie-Victorin, renowned Quebec botanist, meets with Duplessis and proposes the creation of the Montreal Botanical Garden in the east end of Montreal. Duplessis approves. This is a make-work project at a time of wide-spread unemployment.

CANADA AND THE WORLD

1935
Mackenzie King becomes prime minister of Canada for the second time.

Italian troops invade Ethiopia as Mussolini seeks to make Italy into a colonial power.

1936
The Canadian Broadcasting Corporation (CBC) is established.

Léon Blum and his Popular Front win the election in France. The party unites the Left to fight Fascism.

Nazi Germany and Fascist Italy form an alliance.

In Spain, civil war breaks out between Nationalists under General Franco and Republicans.

In the U.S.S.R., Stalin liquidates the Old Guard of the Bolsheviks.

MAURICE DUPLESSIS AND QUEBEC	CANADA AND THE WORLD

Duplessis creates the Provincial Farm Credit program to help the farmers.

Under Duplessis, a law creating Quebec's first old age pension is voted upon and passed.

1937
Duplessis passes an Act Respecting Communist Propaganda, known as the Padlock Law, which forbids the use of one's home to propagate Communism or Bolshevism.

The Quebec Legislative Assembly ratifies the Fair Wage Act and the Needy Mothers Assistance Act.

Brother André dies. During the funeral, Duplessis decides to help fulfil the reverend Brother's life-long dream of building a shrine in honour of his patron saint. St. Joseph's Oratory will rise on the side of Mount Royal and become a symbol of Montreal.

Radio station CKAC broadcasts a program starring Fridolin, the character created by Gratien Gélinas, who is considered one of the founders of modern Canadian theatre and film.

1938
Camillien Houde is re-elected mayor of Montreal.

1937
The Rowell-Sirois Commission is set up to study federal-provincial relations.

In Great Britain, George VI is crowned King.

The Spanish town of Guernica is bombed by German aircraft. The event is immortalized by Picasso in a great painting shown at the World Fair in Paris.

1938
German troops invade Austria. Hitler annexes the country to Germany in the Anschluss, the political union between the two nations.

MAURICE DUPLESSIS AND QUEBEC

Father Georges-Henri Lévesque founds the social sciences department of the Université Laval.

1939
King George VI and his wife, Queen Elizabeth, visit Canada and the U.S.

In October, the Liberal Party under Adélard Godbout wins the election, based on the promise of the federal minister of justice, Ernest Lapointe, that there will be no conscription.

Montreal Mayor Camillien Houde wins in the provincial election as an Independent for the riding of Sainte-Marie.

1940
Adélard Godbout's Liberal government gives Quebec women the right to vote.

Camillien Houde refuses to register for the draft and suggests that the population should follow his example. He is arrested and detained in Petawawa, Ontario.

Monsignor Joseph Charbonneau is named archbishop of Montreal.

CANADA AND THE WORLD

Fearing a major conflict in Europe, France and Great Britain sign the Munich Agreement, giving their consent to Hitler's annexation of the Sudetenland in Czechoslovakia.

1939
The Second World War begins when German forces invade Poland on September 1. France and Great Britain declare war on Germany.

Canada declares war on Germany on September 10. The U.S. remains neutral in the conflict but supplies arms to the Allies.

Generalissimo Franco's forces win the Spanish Civil War.

1940
In the Canadian federal election, Mackenzie King's Liberals are re-elected. The National Resources Mobilization Act requires eligible men and women to register for military service within Canada, for domestic defence.

In Great Britain, Winston Churchill becomes prime minister.

Italy enters the war on the side of Germany.

MAURICE DUPLESSIS AND QUEBEC	CANADA AND THE WORLD
	Belgium, Denmark, Holland, Luxembourg, and Norway are invaded by German troops.
	France surrenders, and Field Marshal Pétain sets up the Vichy government. General Charles de Gaulle calls upon the French to resist. He forms the Free French Army.
	1941 The U.S.S.R. enters the war against Germany.
	On December 7, the Japanese attack Pearl Harbor in Hawaii. The U.S. declares war against Japan and its allies, Germany and Italy. The conflict has become worldwide.
1942 Duplessis undergoes an emergency hernia operation that leads to a four-month convalescence period. He also suffers from diabetes and consumption.	**1942** A plebiscite on conscription is held in Canada. Mackenzie King appeals directly to the citizens. Canada as a whole votes Yes with 63.7 per cent; Quebec votes No with 71.2 per cent.
The Quebec Legislature votes against conscription.	Maxime Raymond founds the Bloc Populaire, a party of Quebecers opposed to conscription. André Laurendeau, the provincial chief, becomes secretary.
1943 Godbout's Liberal government ratifies the Education Act proclaiming mandatory school attendance for children aged 6-14.	**1943** In Canada, the Quebec Conference with Churchill and Roosevelt aims to speed up the preparations for the invasion of Normandy.

MAURICE DUPLESSIS AND QUEBEC

A special commission is created to draw up a proposal for a universal health insurance plan. Duplessis dissolves the commission after his re-election the following year.

1944
The Godbout government nationalizes the Montreal Light, Heat and Power Co. and creates Hydro-Québec. The government also ratifies a new labour code and an act governing working conditions and wage disparities between public- and private-sector workers.

The Union Nationale under Duplessis regains power with only 38 per cent of the vote, as opposed to 40 per cent for the Liberals.

Camillien Houde returns to Montreal after four years of internment.

1945
Premier Maurice Duplessis consolidates his power by personally taking on the offices of attorney general and minister for intergovernmental affairs.

The Quebec government under Duplessis demands from the federal government the right to collect personal and corporate income taxes, as well as inheritance and gasoline taxes.

CANADA AND THE WORLD

1944
In Italy, U.S. forces enter Rome.

On June 6, under the command of U.S. General Dwight D. Eisenhower, the Allies land in Normandy, France. The liberation of Europe begins.

In the Pacific, there is massive intervention by U.S. forces who drive back the Japanese and advance towards Japan.

1945
In Canada, Mackenzie King is re-elected prime minister, with a strong Liberal majority.

Germany surrenders on May 8, bringing an end to the war in Europe. The Allied forces discover the Nazi concentration camps where millions of Jews and other civilians were imprisoned and killed. They rescue the survivors.

On August 6 an atomic bomb is dropped on Hiroshima and

**MAURICE DUPLESSIS
AND QUEBEC**   **CANADA AND THE WORLD**

Duplessis establishes the rural electrification program and the Department of Natural Resources.

another one on August 9 on Nagasaki. Japan surrenders on September 2.

The newly formed United Nations, whose mandate is to maintain peace amongst nations and insure the observance of Human Rights everywhere, meets for the first time.

U.S. President Franklin Delano Roosevelt dies and is succeeded by Harry Truman.

1946
The Duplessis government creates the Social Justice and Youth Department.

In Montreal, restaurant owner Frank Roncarelli posts bonds for the Jehovah's Witnesses Duplessis has arrested for sedition. Duplessis causes Roncarelli's liquor licence to be revoked; Roncarelli takes the premier to court.

1946
War begins in Indochina when France attempts to assert control over its former colony after the Japanese invaders have withdrawn at the end of the Second World War. After France abandons the war effort, the conflict later turns into the Vietnam War, waged by the U.S. against Communist North Vietnam.

Winston Churchill introduces the term "Iron Curtain" to describe the alienation between the Eastern Bloc and the West that is developing into the Cold War.

1947
Hydro-Québec takes over the Montreal Light, Heat and Power Co.

1947
Canada becomes a member of the United Nations.

Great Britain grants independence to India.

MAURICE DUPLESSIS AND QUEBEC

CANADA AND THE WORLD

The U.S. proclaims the Truman Doctrine to stop the advance of Communism and to create the Marshall Plan for the reconstruction of Europe.

1948

After a reconciliation with Duplessis, Camillien Houde becomes Chief Electoral Officer. The Union Nationale wins the election.

Duplessis declares the Fleur-de-lis the Quebec provincial flag, replacing the Union Jack.

The *Refus global* manifest is published, signed by Paul-Émile Borduas and the Young Automatists. It is a fierce protest against a conformist society modelled on outmoded social norms.

1949

The Asbestos strike is a brutal confrontation between workers and management. To Duplessis's surprise, many members of the clergy, among them Monsignor Charbonneau, support the strikers.

Hydro-Québec acquires the properties, factories, and hydro dams along the Ottawa River.

1948

Liberal Louis Saint-Laurent becomes prime minister of Canada.

Mahatma Gandhi is assassinated in India.

David Ben Gurion proclaims the State of Israel.

1949

Louis Saint-Laurent wins the Canadian federal election. The country becomes a member of NATO, the North Atlantic Treaty Organization. Newfoundland becomes Canada's tenth province.

Germany is divided into four zones. The American-, British- and French-occupied zones become the Federal Republic of Germany, integrated into the western hemisphere, and the Soviet zone becomes the German Democratic Republic, integrated into the Soviet bloc.

MAURICE DUPLESSIS AND QUEBEC	**CANADA AND THE WORLD**
	Mao Zedong proclaims the Republic of China.
	Apartheid is introduced into South Africa.
1950	**1950**
Paul-Émile Léger becomes archbishop of Montreal, replacing Monsignor Charbonneau, who resigned his post under pressure from Duplessis.	Communist North Korea attacks South Korea. U.S. forces under General Douglas MacArthur intervene.
Gérard Pelletier and Pierre Elliott Trudeau found *Cité libre*, a magazine that attacks traditional Quebec nationalist themes.	
1952	**1952**
The Union Nationale party under Duplessis wins re-election, with a reduced majority, against the Liberals under George-Émile Lapalme.	In September, the CBC begins operating its first two television stations, CBFT in Montreal (bilingual) and CBLT in Toronto (English). French-language television is broadcast by Radio-Canada, the French department of the CBC.
The Duplessis government creates the Department of Transport.	In Great Britain, Queen Elizabeth II succeeds King George VI.
1953	**1953**
Duplessis refuses subsidies from the federal government for universities because he believes that education must remain in the hands of the Church.	Dwight D. Eisenhower becomes president of the U.S.
	In the U.S.S.R., Joseph Stalin dies.
A royal commission (Tremblay Commission) is constituted with	The Korean War ends.

MAURICE DUPLESSIS AND QUEBEC

the mandate to investigate constitutional issues.

1954

The Quebec provincial government under Duplessis is finally granted the power to collect provincial income tax and forces the federal government to reduce its taxes by 10 per cent.

1956

Maurice Duplessis and the Union Nationale win another mandate.

Duplessis is found to have exceeded his legal authority and is ordered to pay substantial damages to Frank Roncarelli.

1957

The Fédération des travailleurs du Québec (FTQ) [Quebec Federation of Labour] is founded.

Raymond Barbeau founds the Alliance laurentienne, which advocates Quebec independence.

CANADA AND THE WORLD

1954

The war in Indochina ends. Based on the Geneva Accords, Vietnam is divided into North and South Vietnam. War begins in Algeria.

1956

In Hungary, insurrection in Budapest leads to repression by Soviet troops.

In the Middle East, General Nasser's announcement of the nationalization of the Suez Canal by Egypt provokes an attack by Israel on Egypt, and the landing of a French-British coalition force at Suez to protect the canal. The UN intervenes, and Canadian Lester B. Pearson manages to resolve the crisis.

1957

Conservative John Diefenbaker is elected prime minister of Canada. Lester B. Pearson is awarded the Nobel Peace Prize.

The European Economic Community is formed.

The U.S.S.R. launches the first outer-space satellite, Sputnik.

MAURICE DUPLESSIS AND QUEBEC	**CANADA AND THE WORLD**
1959 Maurice Duplessis dies on September 7 in Schefferville. Paul Sauvé succeeds him as premier.	**1959** The St. Lawrence Seaway opens. Fidel Castro defeats Fulgencio Batista and takes power in Cuba. He soon allies himself with the U.S.S.R.
1960 Paul Sauvé dies. Antonio Barrette succeeds him. The Liberals under Jean Lesage win the election and the Quiet Revolution begins.	**1960** Democrat John F. Kennedy becomes president of the U.S. He is the youngest man to be elected president, and the first Roman Catholic.

Sources Consulted

English

BLACK, Conrad. *Render Unto Caesar: The Life and Legacy of Maurice Duplessis.* Toronto: Key Porter Books Limited, 1998

————. *Duplessis.* Toronto: McClelland and Stewart, 1977

Laporte, Pierre. *The True Face of Duplessis.* Montreal: Harvest House, 1970

French

APRIL, Pierre. "Il y a 40 ans, mourait Maurice Duplessis." *La Presse,* September 7, 1999, p. B4.

ARCAND, Denys. *Duplessis.* Montréal: VLB éditeur, 1978.

BARRETTE, Antonio. *Mémoires.* Montréal: éditions Beauchemin, 1966.

BEAUDET, Gilles. *Frère Marie-Victorin.* Montréal: Lidec, 1985.

BLACK, Conrad. *Duplessis.* Montréal: Éditions de l'Homme, 1977: t. 1, *L'ascension*; t. 2, *Le pouvoir.*

CARDINAL, Mario, Vincent LEMIEUX et Florian SAUVAGEAU. *Si l'Union nationale m'était contée.* Montréal: Éditions du Boréal express, 1978.

COMEAU, Paul-André. *Le Bloc populaire, 1942-1948*. Montréal: Québec-Amérique, 1982.

DESROSIERS, Richard (dir.). *Le personnel politique québécois*. Montréal: Éditions du Boréal express, 1972.

DION, Léon. *Les intellectuels et le temps de Duplessis*. Québec: Presses de l'Université Laval, 1993.

FERLAND, Philippe. *Paul Gouin*. Montréal: Québec-Amérique, 1991.

FOURNIER, Me Rodolphe. *Lieux et monuments historiques de Trois-Rivières et environs*. Trois-Rivières: Éditions du Bien Public, 1978.

HÉBERT, Jacques. *Duplessis, non merci!*. Montréal: Boréal, 2000.

JASMIN, Claude. *Le patriarche bleu Duplessis*. Montréal: Lanctôt éditeur, 1999.

LAMARCHE, Jacques. *Les 27 premiers ministres du Québec*. Montréal: Lidec, 1997.

———. Les 20 premiers ministres du Canada, Montréal: Lidec, 1998.

LAPORTE, Pierre. *Le vrai visage de Duplessis*. Montréal: Éditions de l'Homme, 1960.

MARCOTTE, Gilles. *La mort de Maurice Duplessis*. Montréal: Boréal, 1999.

MCDONOUGH, John Thomas. *Charbonneau et le chef*. Adaptation et translation by Paul Hébert et Pierre Morency. Montréal: Leméac, 1974.

MONIÈRE, Denis. *Le développement des idéologies au Québec*. Montréal: Québec-Amérique, 1977.

PROVENCHER, Jean. *Chronologie du Québec*. Montréal: Bibliothèque québécoise, 1991.

RIOUX, Marcel. *Les Québécois*. Paris: Seuil, 1974.

Roy, Jean-Louis. *La marche des Québécois, le temps des ruptures (1945-1960)*. Montréal: Leméac, 1976.

Rumilly, Robert. *Duplessis*, Vols. I et II. Montréal: Fides, 1973.

Saint-Michel, Serge. *Frère André*. Montréal: Safidamédia, 1993.

Tard, Louis-Martin. *Camillien Houde*. Montréal: XYZ éditeur, 1999.

Vastel, Michel. "Le retour de Duplessis." *L'Actualité*, September 1, 1999.

Vennat, Pierre. "Un homme attachant mais parfois dur." *La Presse*, cahier Plus, September 4, 1999.

———. "Il y a 40 ans, disparaissait Maurice Le Noblet Duplessis." *La Presse*, September 7, 1999.

Index

Numbers in *italics* indicate pages with photographs.

Thomson, J.H., 197, 198, 201
Timmins, Jules, 168, 181, 197, 201
Toronto, 104
Tremblay, William, 102, 103, 106
Trempe, Dr. Florian, 142
Trenet, Charles, 180
Trois de Québec, 195
Trois-Rivières, 5, 6, 9, 11, 12, 16,
  19, 22-24, 27-29, 32, 34, 35, 37,
  39-42, 44, 47, 58, 66, 69, 70, 72,
  82, 85, 86, 102, 117, 119, 165,
  166, 175, 192, 197, 204, 206,
  212, 215, 216; great fire of, 11,
  212
Trudeau, Pierre Elliott, 186, 224
Tupper, Sir Charles, 15
Two Mountains riding, 52, 128

ultramontanism, 5, 12, 210
Ungava, 180, 212
Union Nationale Party, 68, 70, 75,
  78-80, 81, 82, 84-89, 93, 98, 101,
  103, 106, 111, 115, 116, 118-
  121, 123, 126-128, 136, 137,
  139, 141, 143, 146, 150, 153-
  155, 157, 158, 159, 162, 163,
  165-168, 170-174, 177, 181, 182,
  187, 188, 189-193, 195, 198,
  201, 202, 204, 205, 207, 217,
  221, 223, 224, 225; founding of,
  67, 217; rural base of, 137, 177,
  192, 195; dissension in, 146, 180;
  by-elections, 198; elections. *See*
  Duplessis, Maurice: election
  campaigns.

unions, 101, 106, 145, 167, 168,
  183, 184, 194
United Press, 189
United States of America, 17, 34,
  95, 98, 136, 140, 151, 167, 180,
  181, 188, 209-212, 216, 219-222,
  224, 226
Université de Montréal, 37, 213
Université Laval; in Montreal, 4,
  12, 13, 212; in Quebec City, 183,
  214, 219
urbanization, 121

Valcartier, 62
Vautrin, Irénée, 73, 77, 78
Venezuela, 102
Villeneuve, Cardinal Rodrigue, 46,
  92-95, 99, 100, 110, 114, 121,
  125, 131, 132, 216
Vineberg, Abel, 58, 59, 74, 75, 88,
  105-108, 117, 132, 153, 165, 190
vote-rigging, 42

Wabasso Cotton Co., 11
War Measures Act, 113
Windsor Station, 63, 160
women's vote in Quebec, 92, 125,
  157, 164, 219

Yamachiche riding, 119
Yamaska riding, 82
Yankees, New York, 27, 28, 59, 91